Interpreting the Lessons of the Church Year

Richard I. Pervo

EPIPHANY

PROCLAMATION 6 | SERIES C

FORTRESS PRESS | MINNEAPOLIS

PROCLAMATION 6
Interpreting the Lessons of the Church Year
Series C, Epiphany

Copyright © 1997 Augsburg Fortress. All rights reserved. Except for brief quotations in critical articles or reviews, no part of this book may be reproduced in any manner without prior written permission of the publisher. Write to: Augsburg Fortress, 426 S. Fifth St., Box 1209, Minneapolis, MN 55440.

Scripture quotations, unless otherwise indicated, are from the New Revised Standard Version Bible, copyright © 1989 by the Division of Christian Education of the National Council of Churches in the U.S.A. and are used by permission.

Cover design: Ellen Maly
Text design: David Lott

The Library of Congress has cataloged the first four volumes of Series A as follows:

Proclamation 6, Series A: interpreting the lessons of the church
  year.
      p.   cm.
    Contents: [1] Advent/Christmas / J. Christiaan Beker — [2] Epiphany / Susan K. Hedahl — [3] Lent / Peter J. Gomes — [4] Holy Week / Robin Scroggs.
    ISBN 0-8006-4207-4 (v. 1 : alk. paper) — ISBN 0-8006-4208-2 (v. 2 : alk. paper) — ISBN 0-8006-4209-0 (v. 3 : alk. paper) — ISBN 0-8006-4210-4 (v. 4 : alk. paper).
    1. Bible—Homiletical use. 2. Bible—liturgical lessons, English.
BS534.5P74   1995
251—dc20   95-4622
                                                                          CIP

   Series C:
   Advent/Christmas / E. Elizabeth Johnson—ISBN 0-8006-4231-7
   Epiphany / Richard I. Pervo—ISBN 0-8006-4232-5
   Lent / Bernhard W. Anderson —ISBN 0-8006-4233-3
   Holy Week / Patricia Wilson-Kastner—ISBN 0-8006-4234-1
   Easter / L. William Countryman—ISBN 0-8006-4235-X
   Pentecost 1 / Terence E. Fretheim—ISBN 0-8006-4236-8
   Pentecost 2 / James L. Boyce—ISBN 0-8006-4237-6
   Pentecost 3 / William L. Holladay—ISBN 0-8006-4238-4

The paper used in this publication meets the minimum requirements of American National Standard for Information Sciences—Permanence of Paper for Printed Library Materials, ANSI Z329.48-1948.

Manufactured in the U. S. A.   AF 1-4232

    01   00   99   98   97   1   2   3   4   5   6   7   8   9   10

Contents

The Epiphany of Our Lord	4
First Sunday after the Epiphany *The Baptism of Our Lord*	11
Second Sunday after the Epiphany *Second Sunday in Ordinary Time*	18
Third Sunday after the Epiphany *Third Sunday in Ordinary Time*	23
Fourth Sunday after the Epiphany *Fourth Sunday in Ordinary Time*	29
Fifth Sunday after the Epiphany *Fifth Sunday in Ordinary Time*	35
Sixth Sunday after the Epiphany *Sixth Sunday in Ordinary Time/Proper 1*	41
Seventh Sunday after the Epiphany *Seventh Sunday in Ordinary Time/Proper 2*	47
Eighth Sunday after the Epiphany *Eighth Sunday in Ordinary Time/Proper 3*	53
The Transfiguration of Our Lord *Last Sunday after the Epiphany*	59

The Epiphany of Our Lord

Lectionary	First Lesson	Psalm	Second Lesson	Gospel
Revised Common	Isa. 60:1-6	Ps. 72:1-7, 10-14	Eph. 3:1-12	Matt. 2:1-12
Episcopal (BCP)	Isa. 60:1-6, 9	Psalm 72 or 72:1-2, 10-17	Eph. 3:1-12	Matt. 2:1-12
Roman Catholic	Isa. 60:1-6	Ps. 72:1-2, 7-8, 10-13	Eph. 3:2-3, 5-6	Matt. 2:1-12
Lutheran (LBW)	Isa. 60:1-6	Psalm 72	Eph. 3:2-12	Matt. 2:1-12

In Western "Christendom" Epiphany is a single feast that concludes the festal period of Christmas. Since the patristic era the focus of this feast has been for the Western church the revelation of Christ to the Gentiles, a message of inclusion that the church has often failed to heed.

FIRST LESSON: ISAIAH 60:1-6, 9

In the background of this exultant hymn lies a long period of bondage and exile, preceded by the desolation and ruin of nation, land, temple, and hope, crushed beneath the inexorable wheels of rapacious and expansive imperialism. No political situations are permanent. The rise of a new empire, under the Achaemenid (Persian) Cyrus, brought changes in policy. Jerusalem and its temple were to be rebuilt as a subject state. Isaiah 60:1—62:12 appears to be hymns composed by the prophet called Third Isaiah shortly after his long-awaited return to the city. The prophet is himself a model for subsequent interpreters, for he applies the oracles of Deutero-Isaiah to the new situation. The glorious new exodus envisioned by Deutero-Isaiah had not quite panned out. These subsequent oracles do not invite the returnees to sit down and weep as they had by the waters of Babylon, but exhort and inspire them toward newer and even greater hopes. The object of prophetic address is the personified land, rather than its inhabitants (v. 6).

The prophecy is, in more than one sense, inspired, for the city seen by this returned exile was no bastion of splendor, certainly not in comparison with world capitols. A supernatural event is in view. Is this to be a politicoeconomic miracle that will make Jerusalem the beneficiary of an enormous trade balance? One may not do the prophet justice by assuming that his images are purely concrete. The splendor of this "new" Jerusalem consists in its character: light. "Glory" is a metonymy for God and a divine gift, illumination. Endowed with this gift Jerusalem will attract the riches of the earth.

The background of this image is also worthy of consideration. "Epiphany" characterized for ancient believers the manifestation of the divine in events that we might call either "natural" or "miraculous." During the Graeco-Roman period the term acquired a connotation of the appearance of that for which people look for to change their troubled lives and times. The religious imagery of ancient Israel exploited the manifestation of a sky-god in a thunderstorm erupting on mountain heights, with fire, thunder, lightning, and smoke. The full repertory of this imagery will appear in the Transfiguration readings, thus bracketing the period between Christmas and Lent with the halves of a divided halo. During the exile, however, the Israelites had experienced other religious symbols, including the basic bipolarity of darkness and light. The prophet has utilized this contrast in his portrayal of a gloom-shrouded world irresistibly drawn to the single beacon of hope.

Jerusalem is to be "a light to the nations," light in the moral sense. This is the imperative—two imperatives, in fact ("Arise, shine"), a construction of which this author is fond. The double exhortation may be a bit more than poetic redundancy. The command is not "fire," but "Ready. Aim. Fire!" The temptation to fire without aiming is strong; witness the number of computer software manuals that presume users will leap into a program without perusing the written instructions. The wake-up call precedes the summons to action. This is so obvious that is does not seem to warrant a mention, but what is most obvious is easily overlooked.

Even more important and more often overlooked is the accompanying indicative: "for your light has come." The light in question is not some neglected natural gift or quality. It is the gift of God. There are defects in the lyrics of the children's hymn "This little light of mine; I'm gonna make it shine." The light is neither little nor mine. That epiphany of which Isaiah 60 speaks is not the result of a thousand or more individual points of light. It is not even personal. The author precludes individual and national claims to be the source of light. This reading establishes in vivid and exultant language the meaning of epiphany. First appears the divine manifestation, then the communal. Its impact will turn the world upside down, making a ruined provincial capital the center of international exchange, shattering expectations and breaking boundaries. Exile is on the way out. Not willing to end there, the author has more imperatives, linked to future indicatives: "Lift up your eyes. . . . Then you will see and be radiant" (vv. 4-5). First you look and then you see. Logical enough. Do you wish to look radiant? This commercial bases radiance in vision, insight, and contemplation. First you look and then you look good. Beauty comes from without, but not without looking. Epiphany is instruction in how to see as well as how to be the light of God in a gloomy world. One of those who understood Isaiah 60 in this way was the Evangelist Matthew.

SECOND LESSON: EPHESIANS 3:1-12

Ascription of authorship in ancient (and medieval) times had more to do with authority and affiliation than with composition. The freshness with which Ephesians addresses issues is more apparent when one does not attempt to make it a paraphrase of what Paul wrote elsewhere. The author could describe the epiphany of Paul's Gentile ministry with much less reserve than the apostle would have exercised. In the liturgical context the significance of this reading is apparent: the inclusion of Gentiles. Yet this author saw the danger that inclusion of Gentiles could lead to exclusion of Jews, which would not be inclusive, and thus understands and proclaims the epiphany of the church as a unity displaying God's plan of salvation for all.

Just as Third Isaiah was an interpreter of the second prophet in that collection, so Ephesians reinterprets Colossians, specifically Col. 1:23-28. This is not mere cribbing. The unit proper extends from v. 1 through v. 13, as the repetition of "therefore" (*dia touto*) indicates. Verses 14 and following show that the author begins an intercession for the community in v. 1 but disrupts it. "We interrupt this prayer to bring you a special announcement." Special it is. The author is not about to hide Paul's unique role as commissioned decoder of divine mysteries under a bushel basket, but the content and ground of this great role is the good news. In what strikes modern readers as rather turgid and verbose language the bottom line is clear and abundant: if Gentiles are heirs of salvation, the realm of darkness and misery has been vanquished. Darkness consists in exclusion, which institutionalizes ignorance. The miracle of inclusion is driven home with three coordinate adjectives formed with *syn-*: "fellow heirs, members of the same body, and sharers in the promise" (v. 6). Mere verbosity? More like hammer-blows shattering the dividing wall (Eph. 2:14). Verses 8-12 contain a related point. Apostolic epiphany—apostolic ministry as revelation—is also a divine gift, exemplified by the credentials of its bearer, Paul, who did not seem the best-qualified candidate. This epiphany is paradoxical, for the mode through which glory becomes manifest is suffering. Its product is the church, itself an epiphany. The result is open access to God (v. 12). On that path of access the light of salvation shines.

Protestant theologians have, in recent decades, reprimanded the author of Ephesians for replacing Christology with ecclesiology, of making the church the instrument of salvation. One should rather, some will say, speak of "the gospel." Such criticism is not without warrant, in particular when the church is living at ease in Zion while guarding its doors, but "the gospel" cannot be proclaimed in a vacuum, either social or intellectual. The ecclesiology of Ephesians is "higher" than Paul's in some ways, as is its Christology. Both seek less to bash outsiders or to lock in God than to assure the community of its empowerment.

Inclusion seem to be a perennial problem for the church. Ephesians shares a Pauline understanding made more explicit in readings assigned for the Sundays after Epiphany from 1 Corinthians 12. Contemporary ecclesiology tends to see inclusion "from below." The more diversity we include and—even more importantly—display, the more closely we shall approximate the body of Christ. For Paul inclusion is "from above." Because we are members of Christ, we can, and must, be inclusive. The miracle has already happened. One task of proclamation is to help believers to gaze upon it and be radiant.

GOSPEL: MATTHEW 2:1-12

Matthew 1–2 bears the inadequate name of "infancy narratives." A leading theme of chap. 1 is Jesus's identity (the Messiah). His place of origin is prominent in chap. 2. One common ancient epistemological principle was that knowledge of origin provided knowledge of essence (cf. John 1:46). Each "scene" of the chapter is associated with scriptural texts:

I. *The Quest of the Magi*
   A. 2:1-6. Journey to Jerusalem   (Mic. 5:1-2; 2 Sam. 5:2)
   B. 2:7-12. Journey to Bethlehem   (Ps. 72:10-11; Isa. 60:6)

II. *The Quest of Herod*
   A. 2:13-15. Journey to Egypt   (Hos. 11:1)
   B. 2:16-18. Slaughter of male infants   (Jer. 31:15)
   C. 2:19-23. Journey to Nazareth   ("Scripture")

This rough outline already reveals how much this chapter foreshadows the Gospel as a whole. Even the infant Jesus has no place to lay his head (Matt. 8:20). Equally apparent are the two characters whose fundamental opposition drives the plot: King Herod in all his power and the powerless baby Jesus. The tale of the Magi is so pleasing to readers of every age, era, and culture that it seems cruel to lash it with the critics' whip, but critical reading is a fundamental preliminary to deeper insight. The story includes two popular motifs, the prediction of a new king by soothsayers and the attempt of a ruler to slay or remove a more or less hidden rival. These motifs can be found in sacred literature (Exodus) and Greek drama (*Oedi-*

pus the King), as well as in folklore. In addition there is a specifically Christian adaptation of a third motif: the adoration by foreigners of a great ruler or benefactor. In attempting to blend these three the narrator gets into difficulty.

This is the solitary passage in the New Testament where "wise men" (*magi*, a word derived from an Iranian priestly tribe) receive a good press. Elsewhere (Acts 8:4-25; 13:1-12) *magi* get to be the "bad guys," and "magic" is roundly denounced. Although many *magi* were jacks of various divinatory trades, these are professional astrologers—not simply casters of horoscopes but attentive astronomers. Astrology was a science in the ancient world. When applied to rulers it was potentially subversive, and emperors took careful steps to ban it, although they might use their own horoscopes for propaganda, as did Augustus. (Patristic authorities were generally alert to the danger that Matt. 2:1-12 might seem to be an endorsement of astrology. They were even more eager to avoid the implication that Christ was subject to astral determinism.)

So a new age is announced by these exotic representatives of all the venerable oriental wisdom that any New Age aficionado might admire. They engage in interpretation, concluding that this new star proclaims a particular royal birth. Exegesis leads to action, a kind of pilgrimage to Jerusalem, where, in all apparent innocence, the astrologers inquire after the new monarch. Herod's intelligence system learned of this inquiry. Duly alarmed, he assembled his intelligence experts and put the question to them. The form of his query indicates that Herod has himself engaged in exegesis, for he speaks not of a king but of "the Messiah" (v. 4). None can fault these scribes on their knowledge, for they know the place and the passage. Otherwise they display no curiosity (just like most subsequent Bible scholars, some will say!). The text adduced by these experts shows just how far from wooden Matthew's biblical "prooftexts" can be, for it contains three (English) words not found in Micah: "by no means," an addition that is by no means insignificant. No less insignificant is the completion of Mic. 5:1 with 1 Sam. 5:2b, by which Bethlehem is quite explicitly designated as the messianic birthplace.

The wily Herod then turns the pious astrologers into covert agents, suggesting that they serve as his forerunners. At this point the star displays navigational qualities, indicating the very house where Jesus lives. To this child they happily offer homage and oblations. Through the more conventional (for Matthew) medium of a dream they are deterred from reporting to Herod. Having played their part, the sages are taken off the board. Pious abomination of narrative vacuums has worked its own wonders here, fixing their number, with some variation, at three, and transforming them into martyred missionaries (Eastern traditions) and kings (in the West, where examples of monarchs bestowing worship and wealth upon Jesus were deemed useful). The traditional Christmas crèche has long been teaching lessons about diversity.

The strangest character in the story is not its star but *the* star. Why, since this phenomenon could point out a specific house, did it first bring the astrologers to Jerusalem? From a narrative perspective the entire involvement of Herod and his scribes is gratuitous. The king is, moreover, quite inept. He would have done well to dispatch spies to follow his unwitting spies. These difficulties show precisely what the Evangelist wished to emphasize and introduce. For inspiration Matthew also exploited inspired texts. Balaam (Numbers 22–24) was an oriental diviner who had forecast a star from Jacob and a scepter from Israel (Num. 24:17). Inspiration for the character of Herod comes from the wicked Pharaoh of Exodus. Such "intertextuality" is, of course, far more than the use of convenient sources. By such means the story of Jesus is integrated into the story of Israel and that story into the whole complex of God's "plan" for the salvation of humankind. Ephesians 3:1-12 and Matt. 2:1-12 are different ways of expounding a similar theme. Narrative exposition and theological reflection can illuminate one another.

Matthew's story is a synecdoche for the Gospel, intimating the fate of Jesus, the role of religious authorities in this fate, and the Gentile mission. The passion, in which Jerusalem will again be upset and become murderous, and where the agent of another king will succeed where Herod failed, is foreshadowed. The gifts of the Magi will be used, so to speak, to bury Jesus, while their joy (v. 10) and worship (v. 11) will be echoed in the resurrection narratives (28:8, 9, 17). Their response to the universal authority of the new world ruler intimates at the beginning what 28:16-20 will authoritatively announce.

Artists have sometimes shown a better grasp of the symbolism than have historical analysts. Ancient exegetes, such as Chrysostom, already saw in the star more than a star, because of its strange motion. Star charts and astronomical history are not the place for modern scribes to look for this beacon of grace. This strange star is at one level a symbol of Christ, an unbounded wanderer who brings light in darkness (Isa. 60:2; Matt. 4:13-17). As a medium of revelation it requires interpretation and response. The astrologers' gifts fulfill Isaiah 60, and prod the imagination, a quality with which "precritical" interpreters were often well endowed. The fruits of their reflections are best known in popular hymns, such as the fourth-century poem of Prudentius ("Sacred gifts of mystic meaning: incense doth their God disclose, gold the King of kings proclaimeth, myrrh his sepulcher foreshows" [trans. *Hymns Ancient and Modern*, 1861]), the evident inspiration for stanzas 2–4 of J. H. Hopkins's Christmas carol "We Three Kings of Orient Are."

The success of this tale from the least storytelling evangelist requires no scholarly endorsement. Why has it been so successful and maintained such a grip upon imagination and sentiment? In part because of its fairy-tale charm, the depiction of a world in which stars move for the convenience of travelers, and exotic characters come from afar to worship a baby of humble birth. Such narrative worlds do not invite readers to wonder what the neighbors might have thought about all this. The world of Matthew 2 is like that of the temptation (4:1-11). Because it is "mythical," it is cosmic, beyond time and space. In short, the revelation of Christ to all is a supernatural event, unlimited in application and appeal. Epiphany is an explosion that ends with a prayer: "Guide us by thy perfect light."

First Sunday after the Epiphany
The Baptism of Our Lord

Lectionary	First Lesson	Psalm	Second Lesson	Gospel
Revised Common	Isa. 43:1-7	Psalm 29	Acts 8:14-17	Luke 3:15-17, 21-22
Episcopal (BCP)	Isa. 42:1-9	Ps. 89:1-29 or 89:20-29	Acts 10:34-38	Luke 3:15-16, 21-22
Roman Catholic	Isa. 40:1-5, 9-11	Ps. 29:1-4, 9-10	Titus 2:11-14; 3:4-7	Luke 3:15-16, 21-22
Lutheran (LBW)	Isa. 42:1-7	Ps. 45:7-9	Acts 10:34-38	Luke 3:15-17, 21-22

The remarks for this and subsequent Sundays are not based upon the concept of an "Epiphany season," but view this period before Lent as "ordinary time," like the Sundays following Pentecost. The Baptism of Christ was, for reasons not as clear as one might wish, the text read in some places in the ancient church on January 6. This event is both the inauguration, in some sense, of a "public" ministry, and an elusive epiphany. Two facts pertinent to this event stand out: that Jesus was baptized by John, and that the emerging church found this most embarrassing, for it seemed to imply that Jesus was a sinful human being and thus promoted what would later be called "adoptionism." Given these difficulties, why did the tradition endure? The answer will reveal the significance of Jesus' baptism.

FIRST LESSON: ISAIAH 40:1-5, 9-11; 42:1-9; 43:1-7

All three choices are derived from the first sections of Deutero-Isaiah (40:1—48:22). Since Christian use of the Hebrew Bible long viewed prophetic texts as forecasts of the coming Messiah, it made no particular difference when the several works were composed. The critical task of appreciating the relevance of texts to their eras of composition prompted and benefited from the recognition that Isaiah 40–55 was written during the 540's B.C.E., following Cyrus's overthrow of the neo-Babylonian empire.

Isaiah 40:1-5, 9-11 (Roman Catholic). This choice arches the bridges presumed to divide Advent from Christmas and Epiphany and clearly points to a beginning by invoking the text used to describe the ministry of John the Baptizer (for instance, Luke 3:4-6). The prologue (vv. 1-11) commissions the prophet in the course of an address to an (angelic?) assembly, who are to rouse personified Jerusalem with words of maternal consolation and promise. A new entry into the holy land is in prospect, this time over a superhighway suitable for the advent of a great monarch. Verse 3 contains two of the most productive phrases of the biblical tradition: "Voice in the wilderness" stimulated the Qumran community, the Baptizer, and Christian reflection upon John's mission; "way of the LORD" depicted the life of people of faith as a journey toward repose rather than as a static posture. Luke adopts this as his preferred term for the Christian "movement" (Acts 9:2, and so forth).

Verse 5 affirms that this royal progress will be a public epiphany. To Christian readers these words ironically foreshadow the two processions that will frame Jesus' ministry in Jerusalem: his strangely regal entrance, and his exit in a Roman military procession. Even epiphanies profit from "advance men." Personified Zion and Jerusalem are therefore exhorted to play this role, high and lifted up on the traditional mountaintop of revelation. From v. 9 comes, via Greek, the verb "evangelize." These personifications make the evangelistic task a corporate and pastoral activity. Verse 11 frames the entire passage with the theme of loving parental care. The chief consolation of earthly shepherds and their flocks is that God is the shepherd of all.

Isaiah 42:1-9 (*LBW/BCP*). In studied contrast to the wilderness voice (40:3) is the silence of idols (41:21-29), who are denounced following a trial of the nations and assurance to Israel (41:1-21). The stage is thus set for the first of the famous Servant Songs, which have provided Christians with christological ideas and credal forms. The extent of this first song and the origin and application of all the Servant Songs has generated scholarly debate. These poems accumulate the virtues of various leaders, including kings and prophets, and of the nation as a whole. Insofar as an individual appears to be described, these virtues may be regarded as synecdoches, the whole represented by its foremost part. From the perspective of Christian theology the qualities are both messianic attributes and the resultant "virtues" displayed by members of Christ's body.

Isaiah 42:1-4 requires the kind of public setting suitable for coronations rather than the private environment of prophetic calls. Although many of the Servant's functions, such as proclaiming justice, are priestly or prophetic, his overall role is regal. This is one way in which the text provides christological "background." Jesus will appear as a Messiah of word and deed, combining, as it were, the roles of judge and prophet. Both Servant and Jesus will, however, sharply fail to match the contemporary expectations of regal behavior, for they will not achieve their goals by the exercise of brute power, nor will their views emerge as royal decrees. The

THE BAPTISM OF OUR LORD

genuine representative of the one who rules human events will not operate like those who imagine that they control our destinies. Even a superficial recollection of ancient monuments devoted to royal exploits will provide some contrast to a champion who cannot break a damaged plant or extinguish a failing candle. Failing that candle may be, yet it will not grow faint, nor will this seemingly weak reed be crushed (v. 4). A new kind of power is in prospect.

The power in question will transform sputtering candles into world-embracing beacons and result in genuine justice and peace. "Blindness" and "imprisonment" are synecdoches for all human suffering, both that wrought by nature and by the wrongs of human hands. This will be a new thing indeed. In place of the victory of Cyrus, Augustus, or America, the faithful may look forward to the triumph of justice.

Isaiah 43:1-7 (Revised Common). Rather than supply direct background for the Gospel, this reading, one of Deutero-Isaiah's finest poetic compositions, hymns the creative and redemptive power and policy of God. This is not to suggest that epiphany is ignored, for the address opens with the traditional reassurance: "fear not." For symbolic evocation there are the water and fire of v. 2, here manifest in their role as metonymies for the demonic. The eschatological trials of water and fire proclaimed by the fiery John at the waters of Jordan will not overwhelm or consume God's elect. Promise, not threat, is the theme, an explicit recognition that responsible contemporary evangelism will not seek to gain a foothold by scaring the hell out of people. Universalism also sounds its loud and clear note here. Verse 6b grounds this universal redemption in the parenthood of God, explicating the meaning of baptismal adoption.

SECOND LESSON: ACTS 10:34-38; 8:14-17; TITUS 2:11-14; 3:4-7

Acts 10:34-38 (*LBW/BCP*). This passage is set in the midst of one of the key sections of Acts, the inauguration of a Gentile mission by Peter, not Paul, through explicit divine direction, not human opportunism, initiated by visions, vindicated by miracle, and ratified by the Jerusalem community (10:1—11:18). Short homilies may seem miraculous. This sermon is short because the Spirit of God makes additional words superfluous (v. 47). Formal parallelism with the Gospel is clear: a religious message validated by an immediate and unexpected intervention of the Spirit. One impulse behind Acts 10 is reflection upon the meaning of Jesus' baptism.

The sermon opens with Peter's confession that he has been converted: "God shows no partiality." As often is the case, these words are followed by affirmation of divine partiality: Divine impartiality means that God has no favored nation or race. The playing field is level—a plain in Luke. The verses selected from this brief summary of Jesus' life and work demonstrate the meaning of his messianic anointing, a message of peace coupled with beneficent deeds of power. Through this ministry the devil suffered a major defeat. The view represented is pre-Lukan in part, but clearly Lukan in its use of "benefactor-language" for Christology. This is an early example of "inculturation," explication of the gospel in language relevant to a social system based upon the obligations of the powerful to use their power to help those in need. An excellent example of the typical social benefactor would be Cornelius, a pious and generous officer of high rank. The world is being turned upside down. Impartial gods can create difficulties for national and social systems.

Titus 2:11-14; 3:4-7 (Roman Catholic). Like the reading from Isaiah 40, this selection preserves the bond between Christmas and Epiphany, with a "replay" of a traditional Christmas "epistle." If Luke displays one type of inculturation of the Gospel in the Graeco-Roman world, the Pastoral Epistles show how political propaganda that portrayed monarchs as manifest gods and saviors could be taken up in the service of Christology, and therefore be challenged. The great epiphany is now the "second coming," but believers are not left powerless. The Pauline understandings of atonement, salvation, and baptism endure, together with some reflections upon their meaning for believers settled in the world. Grace is an epiphany, that is, an eschatological event of universal application. The means of salvation are set forth in a few short, sonorous, and confident phrases.

What are believers to do while awaiting this glorious parousia? What they have by baptism been equipped to do. The terms may seem a bit moralistic, but, when all is said and done, self-control, virtue, and godliness are not abominable concepts. Grace is not only empowerment. It has an educative function, training for a journey. The reference to *paideia* authorizes the use of Greek and Jewish wisdom as instruments of formation, not through exhortation to hoist oneself by the bootstraps, but as gifts of the Spirit. There is limited place for "enthusiasm" in this model, but it pointed the way toward the schoolhouses of faith through which Greeks, Romans, and barbarians would slowly, gradually, and never completely be molded into a new people of faith.

Acts 8:14-17 (Revised Common). "The wind/spirit blows where it chooses" is proclaimed in John 3:8, and as is demonstrated in Acts, where the Spirit may arrive is before, during, or after baptism. For Luke Samaria is the place of "the other," peopled by some who exasperatingly refuse to behave like the other, including good (Luke 10:29-35) and grateful (Luke 17:11-19) examples, as well as those who do meet expectations (Luke 9:52-53). The very notion of evangelizing rather than torching Samaria (Luke 9:54) testifies to the power of Pentecost. To this land of the other both apostles and Spirit come. One utility of this selection is that it speaks only, simply, and directly of the gift of the Spirit, without specifics and without frills. How is this gift manifest? Those who plaster biblical gaps will have no difficulty in finding possible "completions" for the Lukan narrative, but sometimes gaps are best left as gaps. Cornelius will represent the establishment, with all of its grace and resources. These Samaritans have nothing to give and stand forth as one-time aliens and strangers now brought close and incorporated into the community of faith.

GOSPEL: LUKE 3:15-17, 21-22

Luke 3:1-20 summarizes the ministry of the Baptizer, completing the account begun in chaps. 1–2. As there, stories about John and Jesus are paired, to the advantage of the latter. Luke's portrait of John is quite distinctive. The Gospel selection begins after a summary of his teaching, which includes fiery prophecy and a brief ethical catechism. Omission of vv. 18-20 is justified insofar as the biography of John is not the theme of the day. It also eliminates Luke's downplaying of John's role in the baptism, for Luke implies that John was imprisoned at the time. By the addition of v. 15 Luke transforms John's famous saying into a response to the question of whether he was the Messiah. The message of the historical John, difficult to recover from the imprint of Christian tradition, probably did not look to a Messiah but to the final intervention of God. Harvest imagery suggests judgment (cf., for example, Isa. 40:24; 41:15-16). When grain was tossed on a shovel, the lighter chaff fell to the floor, leaving wheat. Wind (*pneuma*) was the agent of separation, that is, judgment; fire was the instrument of disposal—chaff was burned. John probably spoke of God's judgment by wind and fire. Through the addition of an adjective this became the Holy Spirit (*pneuma*). The statement of unworthiness (v. 16) is no less significant a modification, for it suggests that the coming mightier one is a person. Removing sandals and washing feet were among the most servile of deeds. Reflection upon the impact of the pollutants emitted by their modes of transportation on dirt roads will indicate why this was so.

One may thus speak of the manipulation of tradition by Christians. The theological implication is that christological views may be corrected by divine action, that tradition is a living force rather than the mere reiteration of cherished views, including those of John, who is regarded as a great saint and hero of the faith not because he foresaw fully all that would come to pass but because he kept faith even when his personal expectations did not materialize. John said, in effect, "If you think that I'm preaching hellfire and brimstone, wait till you see what comes next!" What came next was the Jesus who invited sinners to eat with him. For many, including no small number of Jesus' subsequent followers, the end of the world would have been preferable to such a revolting development.

For Luke the baptism cannot be, as it is in Mark, a dramatic and surprising revelation of Jesus' identity. Chapters 1–2 are not coy about his status. Verse 21 contains two common Lukan motifs: "all the people," with whom Jesus expresses solidarity, and his habit of prayer. Such motifs serve not only to make theological points and exemplify pious activity; they also link sections of the Gospel, making each part an expression of the whole. "All the people" evokes an earlier epiphany (2:11). Jesus' "hours of prayer" are not odd moments snatched from a crowded schedule. They come at crucial points: 5:16; 6:12; 9:18, 28; 22:41. The evangelist understands that nativity, baptism, transfiguration, and passion are not distinct scenes from the "Story of Jesus" but aspects and elements of one story, the story of salvation.

"Open heavens" symbolize revelation and epiphany, the moment when God will finally respond to the longings of the faithful (Isa. 64:1-3). The descent of the Spirit in Mark appears to be a private epiphany and vision (1:10-11). Matthew portrays it as a public announcement (3:17). The basic contrast is between "You are" and "This is." Luke is a bit ambiguous, but the "bodily form" of the Spirit eliminates the possibility of a "purely subjective experience." The text speaks of two actions: descent of the Spirit upon Jesus and a heavenly voice. Popular tradition has suppressed the simile, and some scholarship has unintentionally contributed to the notion of a talking bird. Despite patient research, the background of the symbol remains somewhat elusive. Pigeons of various breeds played a number of symbolic roles. Christians reflecting upon baptism are likely to remember the emissary of Noah (Gen. 8:6-12). "Like a dove" includes many possibilities. When heaven is open, the doors of imagination and interpretation should not precipitously be closed.

What does the voice from heaven say? Scholarly responsibility impels me to observe that the "Western" text, "You are my son; today I have begotten you," is rather too quickly dismissed. This direct quotation of Ps. 2:7 has a good claim to be the earliest recoverable Lukan text. "Today" is a Lukan *leitmotif* (see below on the Third Sunday after the Epiphany). This reading would further serve to unite Jesus' saving ministry, from Christmas to the cross. Against this reading is its decidedly adoptionist tenor. Many

New Testament texts are equally adoptionist, however. The far-from-adoptionist Hebrews can quote this verse twice (1:5; 5:5), and it coheres with Luke 1:35. Most will, however, prefer the conventional text, which is identical to Mark 1:11. Voices from heaven are, not surprisingly, biblically literate. This is not a direct quotation, but an evocation of several passages, including Ps. 2:7; Isa. 42:1; 44:2; Gen. 22:2; Exod. 4:22, most of which address a personified Israel. "Chosen," "Beloved," "First-born," and "Only begotten" are basically synonymous. The accumulation of epithets and allusions from various portions of authoritative Scripture show that the various threads of the "divine plan" here coalesce. A leading advantage of this traditional reading is its inclusive character, both in the sense of varied scriptural expectations and in its corporate understanding. In the Lukan context it recalls 2:14 (the stem *eudok-*). This reading says by evocation what Luke 24:44-49 spells out: Torah, Prophets, and Writings find their fulfillment here. Whichever variant is preferred, Luke 4 invites readers to understand this as messianic anointing and spiritual empowerment. This is to say that the Evangelist of Year C will provide his own exegesis of the baptism of Jesus. At 23:46 Jesus will return the Spirit here received, while Acts 2 reports the gift of wind and fire to transform the nascent community.

So much for Luke's commendable solutions. The initial question remains: Why did early Christians preserve a discomforting story? Equally pressing is the question of why the subsequent church not only reads but even parades this pericope on a major occasion. Form criticism asks if this is a "biographical" or "cult" legend; in short, a story about Jesus or a story about us. Those who check "cult" answer both questions. The baptism of Jesus explains how believers receive the Spirit at baptism and grounds this in the ministry of Jesus. Galatians 3:26-27—"for in Christ Jesus *you are* all children of God through faith. As many of you as were baptized into Christ have clothed yourselves with Christ"—is another relevant announcement. We proclaim the story of Jesus' baptism less to explain who he is than to proclaim who we are. Subsequent Sundays will spell out some of the implications of this empowerment and incorporation by the Spirit.

Second Sunday after the Epiphany
Second Sunday in Ordinary Time

Lectionary	First Lesson	Psalm	Second Lesson	Gospel
Revised Common	Isa. 62:1-5	Ps. 36:5-10	1 Cor. 12:1-11	John 2:1-11
Episcopal (BCP)	Isa. 62:1-5	Psalm 96 or 96:1-10	1 Cor. 12:1-11	John 2:1-11
Roman Catholic	Isa. 62:1-5	Ps. 96:1-3, 7-10	1 Cor. 12:4-11	John 2:1-12
Lutheran (LBW)	Isa. 62:1-5	Ps. 36:5-10	1 Cor. 12:1-11	John 2:1-11

FIRST LESSON: ISAIAH 62:1-5

Isaiah 62 is a single hymn, of which the reading presents the first two strophes (vv. 1-3; 4-5). As is customary in Ordinary Time, the Old Testament reading resonates with the Gospel. Marriage symbolism supplies the obvious motive. These verses also look back to the Baptism of Our Lord, for they celebrate Jerusalem as God's "Delight" (v. 4; cf. Isa. 42:1; Luke 3:22). The deafening silence of God does not silence the prophet, who, like the parabolic characters of Luke 11:5-8 and 18:1-8, persists to the point of impertinence. The object of prayer is not personal vindication but the honor of Zion and Jerusalem, whose name(s) will presently be changed, a signal of new relationship and altered status. The capitalized epithets in v. 4 represent actual proper names for women. Marriage is one image used for the relationship between God and Israel, taken up later by the church. Feminist exegesis has exposed some of the pitfalls of the imagery, which all must agree is based upon a view of marriage as a relation between quite unequal partners. Ecclesiology based upon a view of the church as a "pure virgin" leaves little room for growth. "Union" is less colorful but less constrained. The union here envisioned is a new relationship. The sentiment evoked is the delight one partner takes in another. Thus, as the secular and religious "holiday season" has passed and the danger of "ordinary time" looms large, the prophet invites believers to discover and delight in the riches of a renewing God, a builder whose works are inexhaustible for those who listen, look, and pray.

SECOND LESSON: 1 CORINTHIANS 12:1-11

Consecutive readings from 1 Corinthians 12–15 will occupy the Ordinary Time Sundays before Lent. 1 Corinthians can be read as a loosely unified treatment of the theme of freedom from the world and freedom within the

SECOND SUNDAY AFTER THE EPIPHANY 19

community. Chapters 11–14 address various aspects of worship life. Paul can be exasperating for a number of reasons. He makes too few positive rulings, yet too many. His theology is always pastoral, but it is always theology even when apparently expedient. He expects believers to be able to work things out for themselves in community. This lack of interest in individuals, coupled with authoritarianism and permissiveness in a theological framework, is for many a disastrous recipe. To top it off, he had the effrontery to write as if he lived in the first century. Some of the least-appreciated teachers are later the most admired. With Paul we are always in school. He does not lecture so much as engage in a dialogue with his students, who have varying social, intellectual, and spiritual gifts. The latter are the specific subject here, raised by his converts, apparently in a letter. The time may be the first century and the place Corinth, but the subjects of unity and diversity and the relation of individual freedom to corporate responsibility are of more than antiquarian interest.

Verses 1-3 present his thesis. Many at Corinth were deeply attracted to what we call "pentecostal" experiences, less as the "religion of the oppressed" than as attainments of the intellectually endowed and socially progressive. Paul neither condemns such experiences nor urges their proliferation. Some doubtless saw such gifts as "proof" that one had been given the Spirit and their absence as, at best, spiritual inferiority. Paul therefore begins by observing that non-Christians may also have ecstatic experiences. The single proof that one has the Spirit is affirmation of a (very simple) creed: "Jesus is Lord" (v. 3). This is a miraculous gift, from which all other gifts flow and to which all are subordinate. The rhetorical structures of vv. 4-6 and 7-11 are patent. The first is triadic, a contribution to what will become trinitarian theology. Each phrase begins an expression of diversity ("varieties") and concludes with stress upon unity ("same"). "(Spiritual) gifts," "services," and "(miraculous) activities" correlate with "the Spirit," "the Lord," and "God," respectively. Verse 7 states that all have spiritual gifts, and why: "for the common good." This can be at variance with the pursuit of individual ambition. There follows a syllabus of nine spiritual gifts. The order is not random. At the top is "wisdom"; glossolalia finishes in the cellar, although many Corinthians would have sent this gift to the Rose Bowl. Paul lists it last because it is the least edifying—community-building—item in the catalog, potentially offensive to outsiders (14:23) and prone to swell the heads of its beneficiaries (13:1). Verse 11 is an inclusion with v. 7, bracketing the entire section with emphasis upon the Spirit as creator of unity, and reminding all that spiritual gifts are not based upon individual ability or merit. Is unity then to result in uniformity? For the answer to this important question come back next week, same time, same station, same Spirit.

GOSPEL: JOHN 2:1-11

John 2–4 sets the tone for response to and testimony about Jesus. The theme of *semeia* ("miracles," possibly, in the source, or "signs," certainly, for the Evangelist) emerges as a tool for explication. After chap. 4 these signs will be the subject of detailed interpretation. Chapter 2 focuses upon two incidents that show the beginning and point to or foreshadow the climax of Jesus' ministry.

One principle of the history of religions is that gods manifest their nature in the type of miracles they work. Polytheism assigns various gods particular roles. Wine-miracles were associated with Dionysos, who brought humans relief from tedium and ecstasy by his gift. In the period of Christian origins some gods advanced their claims for universality and omnicompetence by assuming the roles of others. John 2:1-11 belongs to this milieu through its implicit claims to supersede and surpass polytheist and Jewish religion (vv. 6, 11). Honesty in Jewish-Christian dialogue requires the admission that works like John are frankly supersessionist and derive from situations quite unlike our own, which has witnessed the fruit of supersessionism in the Holocaust.

Since all wonders deal with "nature" in some way, Gerd Theissen proposes the term "gift." The miraculous feedings and this transformation share some characteristics: there is no direct request for intervention, and the event itself is not described, only its result. Through such reserve mystery and spontaneity come to the fore. The failure of wine is reported in a brief genitive absolute, as if it were of no more significance than a sunrise, and the transformation itself is relegated to another prosaic participle. Gift miracles are soon allegorized or treated as symbols for development, a tendency of which this passage is an example. There is some discomfort, not least in circles influenced by pietism, in associating with the miraculous feeding stories a miraculous *drinking* story. Although it is true that wine has long been a staple of the Mediterranean diet, this account does presume a rather boisterous wedding reception. The *maître d'* of v. 10 does not, after all, say, "Your typical host offers a good vintage at first, then, after a few of the less prudent guests have taken a drop or two more than the situation strictly requires, distributes an inferior label." Jewish and Christian apocalyptic visionaries did not neglect the availability of fast and free food in paradise, but some of their most extravagant utterances look forward, in the manner of v. 6, to the coming abundance of wine, an item that poor people did not always possess in sufficient supply.

Form criticism, like the feet of Cinderella's stepsisters, establishes what is typical so that the atypical may stand out. As a miracle story intended to establish the credentials of a new god or hero, John 2:1-11 is a fizzle. The narrator does not even indicate that the guests had become aware of this domestic crisis, let alone that a miracle had given them more wine than a cohort of soldiers could imbibe. To whom did Jesus "reveal his glory"? What does the statement that his disciples "believed" in him mean? Had they not believed in him previously? (see 1:19-51). They were not, as in the feeding stories, witnesses to the wonder; nor were they the distributing ministers, who alone were partial to the wonder here (v. 9). Those who fill in these gaps are composing a different story from that of the Evangelist.

The point of the story emerges in v. 10: contrary to ancient expectations, the best comes last. The passage has become something of a pronouncement story, although the pronouncement does not come from Jesus. Verse 10 may be a reflection upon sayings contrasting old with new wine (cf. Mark 2:22). What such guests whose tongues had not become too jaded knew was that the better wine had come later. The thrust is toward Jesus as the bringer of new revelation. It is not correct to say that Jesus manifested his glory and incited faith through transforming water into wine. This apparently transparent story is rather subtle. When new wine appears, its character as revelation is visible only to the eyes of faith. The Evangelist will make this point more than once, climactically in 20:29.

Behind "the first" of v. 11 stands an anarthrous *arche*. In one sense this represents a tension between seeing the "beginning" as the onset of Jesus' ministry (cf. 1 John 1:1-4) or as the absolute beginning of John 1:1. Presuming that the author was aware of this dissonance, one may suspect that this is one more provocative Johannine ambiguity designed to make hearers of the Gospel think. Like the next episode, it also points to the end, evoked by the opening phrase, "on the third day," which, while doubtless continuing the temporal markers of chap. 1 (vv. 29, 35, 43), was not a figure that early Christian readers would overlook. Also pointing to the end is the anonymous mother of Jesus, who will next appear at the foot of the cross (19:26). Their brief and elusive dialogue about the hour is immediately relevant in that it affirms that miracle-workers cannot be manipulated, but for the Fourth Gospel, the Hour of Jesus is his passion (7:30; 12:23; 13:1; and so forth).

Wine was a common symbol for ecstasy and thus for revelation, inspiration, and insight (*in vino veritas*). Moses had sweetened and supplied water in the wilderness (Exod. 15:25; 17:6). Wine, it need not be said, goes him one better. The reference to "Jewish rites of purification" (v. 6) sets the stage for replacement of such rites, domestic here, national in the following "cleansing of the temple." Weddings are a frequent trope for eschatological joy and celebration (Isa. 62:3-5). This rich repertory of symbols presents proclaimers with an opportunity for developing this passage's leading point: the best is yet to come for those who see with the eyes of faith. Is the symbolism sacramental? Probably only in a secondary sense. John is no less elusive about sacraments than about many other matters, although this Evangelist alone develops the symbol of wine (chap. 15, which is rather more clearly sacramental).

Still, such stories appear undesirable to many because they are escapist fantasies that detract from the miseries of the present world, where many lack bread, let alone such frivolities as wine, which is more likely to be a problem for the poor than a boon. The "Protestant work ethic," like classical Marxism, takes a dim view of escapism, convinced that only hard work together with strong faith can achieve anything. Modern and even postmodern thought is likely to give dreams higher marks than either Marx or the Calvin of caricature. Dreams, as those apocalyptic visionaries who wrote about the enormous vines of heaven also realized, can empower. Epiphany visible to the eyes of faith is a good theological phrase, but most need a medium to stir up that vision. Cana is one such recipe for proclaimers. Take a jigger of theology, add a dream, shake vigorously and then present this elegant aperitif, followed by a suitable entrée: the bread of heaven and the cup of salvation. For most of us much of the time the Scriptures and rites of the church seem to be little more than gallons of water, no doubt useful for cleansing, but no more interesting for all that. One priestly task of preachers is to transform that water of blandness into the new wine of revelation, or better, to show that what we think of as mere H_2O is in truth the very water of life, in which, to build upon the previous Sunday, we have been reborn and renewed by the Spirit of God.

Third Sunday after the Epiphany
Third Sunday in Ordinary Time

Lectionary	First Lesson	Psalm	Second Lesson	Gospel
Revised Common	Neh. 8:1-3, 5-6, 8-10	Psalm 19	1 Cor. 12:12-31a	Luke 4:14-21
Episcopal (BCP)	Neh. 8:2-10	Psalm 113	1 Cor. 12:12-27	Luke 4:14-21
Roman Catholic	Neh. 8:2-4, 5-6, 8-10	Ps. 19:8-10, 15	1 Cor. 12:12-30 or 12:12-14, 27	Luke 1:1-4; 4:14-21
Lutheran (LBW)	Isa. 61:1-6	Psalm 113	1 Cor. 12:12-21, 26-27	Luke 4:14-21

FIRST LESSON: ISAIAH 61:1-6; NEHEMIAH 8:1-10

Isaiah 61:1-6 (*LBW*). The motive for this selection is, obviously, to present the Scripture read by Jesus in his inaugural sermon. If the repetition seems redundant, so be it, for these famous words can be savored repeatedly and remain fresh and exciting at every new encounter. Synonymous parallelism, abundant here, has the advantage of saying more or less the same thing in two ways, making each different and neither completely sufficient. So it is with repetition. To paraphrase Heraclitus: one cannot step into the same biblical passage twice. The text therefore reminds us that the assembly at Nazareth and those of our day cannot step into the same waters that flowed from the mouth of Third Isaiah. The entire passage, part of a unit extending to v. 11, is not only rich with vivid images; it is also, especially in vv. 1-3, rich in allusions to other biblical texts, Deutero-Isaiah in particular.

This history of revelation exhibits a gradual democratization of the gift of the Spirit, first a quality the monarch would receive, ultimately an endowment for the entire people (Isaiah 11; Joel 3). Although "anointing" here is a trope for an interior gift, "Spirit" has as its primary reference the might acts of God. The "gospel message" for which the prophet is commissioned is rather class-conscious. We tend to regard the oppressed as a political category and brokenheartedness as emotional. Not so this prophet. Verse 2 has a third member: comfort for mourners (cf. Matt. 5:4). This verb "comfort" ignites the poet to envision a coming transformation, depicted in the common image of changed clothing. Those once ground down now stand proud and tall, prompting comparison to mighty oaks, who, lest they forget, are the fruit of seed sowed by God. Images from nature give way to the products of culture: trees are fashioned into logs and these into buildings, urban ruins are transformed into pleasant habitations. By v. 6 the captive slaves of v. 1 enjoy the ministrations of others, leaving them free to be a priestly community, devoted to God's service. This acquisition of slaves makes liberals cringe (including the rather liberal Jesus of Luke, who ends his text in the middle of this verse), as does the parallelism of "the year of the LORD's favor" with the day of God's vengeance (v. 2). The Bibles of liberation theology are likely to print these unpleasant words in red letters. They are not unhealthy reminders about the realities that true justice entails. Fantasies of vengeance we all have, and shall have. These are natural. What requires grace is to leave vengeance to God, as does our prophet.

Nehemiah 8:1-10 (Roman Catholic/*BCP*/Revised Common). Episcopalians alone offer hearers the entertainment and lectors the challenge of that long list of names, and this not once but twice. A major reason for selecting this text is to provide occasion for reflection upon the public reading of Scripture. In the background is an oral culture, in which books were scarce and private and silent reading was exceptional. Teachers would read the authoritative text, then offer their comments. Today many can "read along" from distributed bulletins or other texts. Useful and convenient as these are, they may detract from listening as a corporate, community-building experience. Examination of 1 Timothy 2 in my private study is a different experience from hearing it read aloud in a public assembly that includes a number of women; the experience of the latter impacts the former.

This passage seems to have been displaced. Its full range runs from 7:73b—8:12. The solemnity of the setting, underscored by repetition, is apparent. Ezra, flanked by six worthies on either side, proclaims (a portion of) the Torah to a large assembly, notable not only for its endurance, but also for its inclusiveness—men, women, and children of sufficient years—and yet more notably, for its initiative. The impetus for this ceremony came "from below." Reading requires interpretation, followed by adoration, and climaxed by celebration. This is what Christians continue to do: proclaim, interpret, worship, and share. The reading of Torah was, and is, "gospel," not just "law." Ezra did not reject repentance, but he demanded celebration as well. Just as the latter is defective without the former, so the former issues in the latter.

SECOND LESSON: I CORINTHIANS 12:12-31a

(For the context, see the introduction to 1 Corinthians 12–15 in the comments regarding the Second Sunday after the Epiphany.) The apostle continues his reflections on unity and diversity. In 1998 this Sunday will close the annual Week of Prayer for Christian Unity. 1 Corinthians 12 provides a

most appropriate occasion for reflection upon the ecumenical movement. If some of the optimism about formal church unions has faded, ecumenism has taught us that the various Christian denominations and bodies are also a *gift*, means of learning from the particular emphases, values, and practices of other groups. Ecumenism based upon uniformity of practice, structure, or belief is always in danger of becoming a quest for the lowest common denominator. Ecumenism that emphasizes organizational (or, less kindly, bureaucratic) amalgamation is always in danger of neglecting the source of unity, God. Ecumenism based upon whatever sharing is possible amidst the recognition that none have all the answers and that each tradition has gifts without which others would be impoverished is not unlike the kind of unity envisioned by Paul.

Pluralism and diversity are also very much a part of contemporary public discourse. Paul is quite willing to use political language and models. Differentiation exists, the apostle affirms, even if it belongs only to this world. Ancient thought looked at unity and diversity in terms of the one and the many, nearly always regarding the one as ultimate, superior, and original. A venerable solution to differentiation is to assign to certain roles and qualities a higher status. Paul, like modern critics of "hierarchy," stoutly resists this, but without dissolving rank or difference. His portrait of the "body politic," set forth in vv. 12-27, was an image of which ancient writers were fond. They used this comparison of the social body to the human body to justify social hierarchy. Toes should rejoice at the knowledge that the body could not run without them; they should not try to play brain but gladly submit. Such bodies come from the masterful assembly of diverse parts. For Paul the body in question is that of Christ. It is *a priori*. Differentiation is subsequent and thus secondary (v. 12). The body of Christ is not a voluntary or involuntary social organization but a supernatural creation. The basis of entry is baptism (v. 13; cf. Gal. 3:26-28). Baptism is sacramental, therefore eschatological, admitting no important differences. In this life, however, the body does exhibit differences, a subject calling for some comment.

Paul's interpretation, playing with the traditional differentiation of limbs and organs, agrees that these cannot set up shop for themselves. "Out of the body" is two-edged, for it refers both to individualism and to ecstasy, the boasts of some who claim that their spiritual gifts have allowed them to escape from the body's constraints. "Body" likewise plays with individual bodies and the *Corpus Christi*. All believers are charismatics by virtue of the gift of the Spirit (vv. 1-3), which brings the possibility of corporate life. All roles and functions are socially and spiritually valid. Even hairs are heirs of eternal life. The apostle does not blast some Corinthians for their "pentecostal" behavior. What he attacks is elitism that draws one away from the life of Christ's body. This cannot be spiritual. The real miracle is not disembodiment; it is incorporation. What that means will be the subject of 1 Corinthians 13.

Rank does exist for "apostles, prophets, and teachers," whose vocations are affirmed. Beyond that there are many functions, but none can claim priority. Those who wash the dishes do more than serve their betters, for their ministry is also a gift. Nearly every present-day church member may find something offensive in these words, including those who use menial service as an indirect route to power, those who cling to simple authoritarian models, those who regard noncharismatics as non-Christians, and, not least, those who would fashion unity by diversity "from below," as if the inclusion of one of this and one of that race, sex, orientation, disability, occupation, age group, and so forth could build the kingdom from the ground up. The result is more likely to resemble the tower of Babel. A more orthodox Christian approach is to take the imperative of comprehensiveness from the indicative of salvation, to say that, because we are the body of Christ, we can and therefore shall be inclusive, that Pentecost, not Babel, is our model.

GOSPEL: LUKE (1:1-4); 4:14-21

The Roman Catholic assignment of the preface to Luke recognizes that it is in Ordinary Time that the featured Synoptic Gospel of each year is experienced in more or less consecutive order. The preface to Luke shows the church placing its feet onto the soil of ordinary life and time, for prefaces belong to certain types of "literature." This preface asserts that the anonymous author is aware of other accounts, upon which he hopes to improve and that he will be pleased to replace. The Holy Spirit guided the church into acceptance of four Gospels. Neither Luke nor Matthew (nor John) envisioned believers making invidious, but illuminating, comparisons among them. Those superficially acquainted with ancient literature see in this preface the claim to be writing history. The Gospel of Luke is more like biography than history, and the language has much in common with technical works on such subjects as animal husbandry or dream-interpretation.

The work has a dedicatee, Theophilus, "friend of God." He is no disinterested outsider, but an informed and instructed person, probably a believer, who is ready for some continuing education. Patristic and medieval commentators already urged readers of the Gospel to assume the role of Theophilus and count themselves among the friends of God privileged to share its message. Modern literary discussions of the "implied reader" say much the same thing.

THIRD SUNDAY AFTER THE EPIPHANY

A traditional approach to the structure of Luke designates 4:14—9:50 as the "Galilean Ministry." This outline derives from Mark 4:1-13, 16-30, and 31-42 present three parallel episodes with a cumulative effect. One may thus, with Frederick Danker, speak of vv. 14-30 as a "Temptation at Nazareth." The passage is nonetheless a beginning, the first public appearance of Jesus. For this inaugural address Luke provides a dramatic story that foreshadows not only the fate of Jesus but also that of his followers, the story of Luke and the story of Acts. This is thus a ideal and typical scene, ideal in so far as it lacks some realism, typical in that it is the single example of what Luke presents as an important component of Jesus' ministry: preaching in synagogues. Since the only apparent source is Mark 6:1-6a, scholars regard this as Lukan composition. The author's method resembles that of Acts; it is a formal speech in a narrative setting. To a degree the division of this text into two weeks is thus inconvenient, for it disrupts the unity of the story. Dramatically, however, this liturgical division offers suspense. The faithful must return next week to learn the outcome. Theologically it lacks nothing, for the climactic verse is an announcement of salvation.

Writers often follow a detailed episode with a summary, suggesting that the incident treated is a typical example. In this instance Luke begins with a summary report. Undeterred by the devil's onslaughts, Jesus, "filled with the power of the Spirit" (a flashback to the baptism [3:21] and to 1:35), preaches with great success. Powerful deeds and powerful words are equally miraculous. The hero enters the town where he was reared. What will be the result? With a confidence that brooks no rejection, Jesus assumes the role of proclamation. Verses 16b-20a are an elegant chiastic composition of thirteen parts. Many ancient readers would appreciate such niceties. The effect is both sonorous and suspenseful. By this act the mature Jesus appears to his public as a person of education and culture. The ability to maneuver through a scroll required considerable training. Were these bookish skills followed by instruction in rhetoric? For the answer to this question one will have to wait.

The narrator is not interested in any "lectionary system," nor in a prior reading from the Torah. Jesus selects his text. Scholars will quickly point out that this text would not be found in a conventional roll of Isaiah, for it is a combination of Isa. 62:1-2, with an omission, and Isa. 58:6, with a modification; in other words, this is a Christian text. The central and emphatic point of that thirteen-part chiasmus lies in v. 18d: sight for the blind. Light and sight are key images bracketing Luke and Acts (cf. Luke 1:79, the *Benedictus*; 2:30-32, the *Nunc Dimittis*; Acts 13:47; 28:26-28, all linked to Isaiah). Its climax is the "year of Jubilee," God's great evener-upper.

The reading finished, Jesus relinquishes the scroll and assumes the sitting posture of a teacher. This is not another ho-hum conclusion of an indifferently read lesson. With the statement that he was the cynosure of all eyes the narrator shows the impact of potent declamation (and nicely picks up the central image of sight). At this moment of great excitement Jesus drops his bomb: all these words, the intense concentration of personal and national hope, are fulfilled. For Christian hearers this includes the understanding that the "me" anointed is Jesus, the Messiah. What of those other fine phrases? Are they simply metaphorical? They are both literal and metaphorical. Exclusion of either would be reductionistic. "Good news" has an object: the poor. Its content is not bliss in heaven someday, but freedom and justice, matters both spiritual and physical, for their spiritual quality assures us that God has more in store than we can ask for or imagine, that even the legitimate aspirations of the poor do not exhaust the possibilities of grace.

The time of fulfillment is not by and by, but rather sooner—"today," to be precise. And now, dear preacher, reach for your concordance and look up "today" in Luke. This is quite a prosaic word, with no hint of Hebrew verbal dynamism or innuendo of Greek metaphysical speculation. There are eleven or twelve uses, the first in 2:11, the angelic announcement of Christmas. Interesting. The last use comes in the words to the thief on the cross. *Very* interesting. There is also a possible use in 3:21, the acclamation in 5:26, and intimation of the passion at 13:32-33. Luke 19:5 and 9 report a different sort of healing, salvation for wealthy Zacchaeus. "Today" is one of those words by which Luke binds his message together and through which he presents various aspects of the single and present event of salvation. Linger for a space over those passages, for there may be a sermon lurking in that little word, a sermon for, of all times, today (note also Jer. 1:10).

"Hearing" is the last word, but not the least. Proclamation begins with prayer that the preacher may learn to listen, so that the ears of hearers may be opened to discovery. Lectionary exigency makes this Gospel a one-sentence sermon. What has Jesus said? Very little and very much. Every good sermon consists of one sentence. Less can sometimes be more, especially when that single sentence becomes lost in the shuffle. Preachers do require a full deck, but our job is to point out that God has dealt our hearers an ace, rather than to talk about what we have discarded or cards we might play or have been dealt by the scoundrels who design lectionaries to frustrate faithful clergy.

Fourth Sunday after the Epiphany
Fourth Sunday in Ordinary Time

Lectionary	First Lesson	Psalm	Second Lesson	Gospel
Revised Common	Jer. 1:4-10	Ps. 71:1-6	1 Cor. 13:1-13	Luke 4:21-30
Episcopal (BCP)	Jer. 1:4-10	Ps. 71:1-17 or 71:1-6, 15-17	1 Cor. 14:12b-20	Luke 4:21-32
Roman Catholic	Jer. 1:4-5, 17-19	Ps. 71:1-6, 15-17	1 Cor. 12:31—13:13 or 13:4-13	Luke 4:21-30
Lutheran (LBW)	Jer. 1:4-10	Ps. 71:1-6, 15-17	1 Cor. 12:27—13:13	Luke 4:21-32

FIRST LESSON: JEREMIAH 1:4-10, 17-19

The call of Jeremiah extends from v. 4 to v. 19, interrupted by a vision in vv. 11-16. The Roman Catholic division focuses upon God's promise to Jeremiah. According to the superscription the call took place c. 627 B.C.E. Jeremiah thus enjoyed—better experienced—a prophetic career of nearly half a century, rather above the average for this high-risk profession. The story begins, quite properly, at the beginning. In view is, of course, the inception of another, much shorter, prophetic ministry, that of Jesus.

Among the qualifications for prophets was a proper call, which included a statement of disqualification. These calls are not public epiphanies but private experiences, often in a state of trance. They do not report simple orders to start prophesying, but include a dialogue. This feature merits attention, suggesting as it does that vocation involves dialogue and even possibly that the oracles and utterances of prophets are incentives to dialogue. Calls are not simply calls; they are also commissions that include empowerment as well as authorization. Of the various prophetic call-stories (see also Isaiah 6, next week's first lesson in most lectionaries) that of Jeremiah holds pride of intertextual place in the New Testament. Paul turned to it to describe his own vocation (Gal. 1:15-16), and Luke (who also shapes the Annunciation, 1:26-39, as a prophetic call) used it to transform the conversion of Paul (Acts 9) into a call story (Acts 22 and 26).

Accounts of prophetic vocation clearly establish the source: divine election, not human initiative. For this purpose any objections offered by the one called serve to strengthen the case. God can work with rather frail vessels. This is precisely the imagery implied in the "formed" of v. 5, a word taken from the potter's craft. Creation, election, consecration, and commission are different aspects of a single act, according to that verse, which provides more than a little clay for the theologian's wheel. This youth will be a prophet to the nations. The prophets did not work in a vacuum. The tangled politics of the ancient Middle East would have prevented this. From the negotiations, concessions, and compromises required by their environment, prophets were discouraged from forgetting that God is Lord of all history.

That Lord brushes off Jeremiah's protestations of immaturity with simple declarations, only then followed by a vision of words placed in his mouth. The middle set of English infinitives in v. 10 ("to destroy and to overthrow") may be a subsequent addition. Without them there is a nice chiasmus: pluck up, pull down, build, plant—a potent set of images. Let the power of these few words roll about the tongue as inspiration for a few well-chosen words of your own. These are enough words to clarify the prophetic task as more than nurture and edification. When the church dodges plucking up and demolition, there will be no construction or planting. Cultivation without digging up is cheap grace. Weeding without sowing denies the possibility of grace. Christians have tried both options, and the results are manifest. Like Jeremiah, the church is summoned to the dialogue between these polarities. Dialogue requires that all be heard, that everyone speak, and that each listen.

God has the final word in vv. 17-19. The prophet is to "hike up his skirts," or, as we say, "roll up his sleeves" and get to work. Breakdowns are not permitted. This is rather grim and unpastoral, but those elevated skirts come equipped with their own supply of strong images: "fortified city, iron pillar, bronze wall," reverberant metaphors that will acquire irony in the light of Jerusalem's ultimate experience. Augustine, the late Bishop of Hippo, who experienced a siege of his own, would have no difficulty in identifying this city. It is the city of God.

SECOND LESSON: I CORINTHIANS 12:27—13:13; 14:12b-20

1 Corinthians 12:27—13:13 (*LBW*/Roman Catholic/Revised Common)
(Comments on 12:28-30, the inclusion of which helps to establish the context of this excursus, community life rather than individual virtue, may be found in the discussion of the second lesson for the Third Sunday after the Epiphany, above).

After listing a number of mainly spectacular gifts, Paul promises something even better. There is no need of a biblical scholar to say that 1 Corinthians 13 is a literary and moral success. Success has dulled its edge and blunted the point. Clergy may shy away from eschatology, but advertisers do not: "This is as good as it gets." For some in Corinth the achievement of certain spiritual gifts was as good as it got. In the teeth of what he

FOURTH SUNDAY AFTER THE EPIPHANY

views as arrogant elitism Paul will introduce spiritual gift number one. Since the discussion of these gifts continues in chap. 14 without ado, this is a disruption of sorts, but quite possibly one of the apostle's own devising, a most elegant digression. The rhetorical embellishments of chap. 13, apparent even in English, are not mere display. These certainly serve, as history has demonstrated, to transform what could be a jejune theme into unforgettable words. They also play to the very audience Paul had in mind, those men and women enamored of "wisdom" and rhetoric (1 Corinthians 1–4). With these memorable paragraphs he will "hook" them to his side so that, in chap. 14, he may push and stretch their horizons.

Parallels, such as 1 Esd. 4:34-40, indicate that this is a prose hymn celebrating the most important deity, virtue, or quality. The first seven verses take up a standard tactic: the virtue in question ("love") is the *medium* through which other commendable virtues find expression. The strength of this approach is that it does not put down other virtues. At v. 8 there is a shift toward polemic, argument that love is not simply the necessary catalyst but the leading virtue. What is the criterion? Eschatology, of course, what is left when all the defects of temporality, motion, plurality, and wickedness have been sifted out and burned. At least some members of the community viewed glossolalia as a real taste of heaven, the language of angelic adoration. No, says the apostle. Ecstasy is temporal as well as temporary. He drives home this startling inversion of values with his plays on the child vs. adult and shadow vs. reality themes so beloved of mystics and philosophers (vv. 11-12), hinting that speaking in tongues may be infantile babble. There is but one eschatological gift, one endowment that is neither transitory nor obscure, possessed by believers in this world. This is the only gift that does not detach believers from the body, for it makes life in that body possible. Here Paul presents his doctrine of justification by faith in social terms, his eschatology in the language of immanence, his ethics stripped of historical limitations. Really?

This Pauline notion of *agape* as the mode through which Christian life takes its form is limited, as some feminist critics astutely note. Behind it stands androcentrism. This is true, from the historical perspective, in that friendship, essentially a male activity, made society possible, and, from the general perspective, in that it addresses a male problem. Women, critics urge, have been taught quite enough about the sacrifice of self for another. *Agape* is a requisite for societies that privilege autonomy, competition, and independence, by and large traditional male pursuits. For women of the present day, at least, the leading issue is acceptance of self.

These observations have force, not least in that they apply not only to women but to most religious persons and all but universally to the clergy.

The result is that *agape* has been transformed into an endorsement of passive aggression and a route to the indirect assertion of power. Paul is no doubt part of "the problem," for he was human, but he did not see love as always caving in to others. 1 Corinthians alone will illustrate that. Verses 4-7 are not an invitation to a "nicey-nice" facade. They are instruments of power that will not leave losers angry and deprived. They are tools for planting that will not be invasive and for uprooting that will not destroy. 1 Corinthians 13 has been the victim of massive and enduring abuse. Church leaders have the responsibility for its rehabilitation. One means lurks in the good old King James Version: "charity." All modern translations prefer "love," and for good reason, but that old rendering reflects that, for ancients, love was not primarily an emotion or a sentiment, but willingness to take responsibility for a need.

1 Corinthians 14:12b-20 (*BCP*). With this selection the *Book of Common Prayer* lectionary relates all three readings to the subject of prophetic vocation. To Paul the criterion for evaluating spiritual gifts is their potential for edification, strengthening the body, rather than what they do for individual self-fulfillment. For an era in which self-fulfillment may seem to be the only norm and discovery of the child within us the leading sign of development, these are harsh words, but they are not entirely without merit. In the background stand two subjects: theories of inspiration and glossolalia. The latter is widely attested and is not limited to religious contexts. For religious individuals the gift is assurance that God has adopted them, a fact that may indicate that other believers have not done their best to make this clear. Ancients debated whether inspiration derived from full possession by a deity or had a human component. In response to the second-century Montanist movement the church rejected the view that claims to inspiration were unimpeachable, but it resurfaced during the nineteenth century in the forms of biblical and papal infallibility.

Paul accepts, perhaps for strategic reasons, the view that "inspiration" is due to the invasion of a divine force that takes over its subject, but he turns it upside down, ranking rational discourse (*nous*) over spirit (*pneuma* viewed as ecstatic possession). What better proof could be offered that the apostle was an Anglican? The edification he has in mind is neither that internal to the recipient nor that internal to the community. "Outsiders" are to be considered, both for the sake of the church's reputation and for its mission. Ancient urban life allowed little privacy. Christians could not conduct their meetings in anything approaching complete secrecy. Did this proto-Anglican really speak in tongues more than these converts he is addressing, or is this a bit of rhetorical fiction? Yes and yes.

FOURTH SUNDAY AFTER THE EPIPHANY

The broader questions present here relate to worship and mission ("inculturation" in current jargon)—to worship as both intellectual and emotional activity, and to the place of "interpretation," none of them minor or out of favor. The historic Anglican tradition and gift has seen, as did its forebears in late antiquity and the middle ages, worship as inculturating, rational, with emotion oriented toward aesthetics. These values are under fire, and not without reason, but dialogue does not proceed on the basis of uprooting and tearing down alone. If the priestly and prophetic task of interpretation is taken seriously, preachers will not take a dive on obscure texts that may confuse or offend. Growth is our goal, wherever and however we start.

GOSPEL: LUKE 4:21-32

(For the context of this continuation, see the discussion of the Gospel for the Third Sunday after the Epiphany, above.) Verse 22 indicates that v. 21 is a summary of Jesus' message, a one-sentence summary of his one-sentence sermon. The news is good, as is its bearer. In v. 22 the narrator gives us the "first reviews," which are quite positive. With them comes a question: "Is this not Joseph's son?" If the answer seems clear—and wrong—the question is open-ended, possibly amazement that the whelp of a local artisan family displays such talent, possibly doubt that the anointed one of whom Isaiah spoke could be the product of a local artisan. The narrative resolves this by turning the sermon into a dialogue, as it were. Jesus supplies them with proverbs as ammunition against him, as well as a demand for more than verbal displays. The first suggests that healing begins at home, with the implication that he is not in the best of mental health. The next saying indicates that healing should begin at home by taking care of its own needs, rather than lavishing the benefits it has taken a village to produce upon such foreign fleshpots as Capernaum. The third clinches the list with Jesus' own interpretation of the prophetic vocation. Now it is clear why we hear earlier of Jeremiah's call. God commissions prophets "to the nations." Other nations have no interest. Their own nation takes offense.

Just whose team God favors, home or away, becomes clear in two illustrations from Bible history. Elijah and Elisha were not only prophets who denounced foreign nations, they also worked great deeds in Capernaum, as it were. The home team does not take this sitting down. False prophets, defined as those who do not say "Peace," whatever the circumstances, threaten civilization as we know it. Scripture is very clear about how to dispose of them. Lynching was not rough, spontaneous justice but response to contamination that defiled the entire community, all of whom had responsibility for prompt and thorough cleansing. The cliff from which this mission was to be accomplished is less a feature for archeologists to locate and pilgrims to admire than it is an allusion to vv. 9-13: Temptation at Nazareth. Who was tempted and how? Jesus and his fellow townsmen. What is the result? He goes on to the despised Capernaum, as he will move from frying pan to frying pan until he plunges into fire at Jerusalem.

If the congregation here has proven to be a disorderly lot, so is the narrative, with its twists, turns, and mysteries. Luke wished to blend triumph with rejection, not only to show that Jesus was not run out of town because he was an oratorical flop, but also to foreshadow the rejection and triumph of his entire ministry. That ministry includes the future community, which is why the scene evokes the fate of Stephen (Acts 6–7) and of Paul (Acts 9–28). The examples are not random; they speak of Gentiles, the favorable mention of whom makes the crowd murderous (cf. also Acts 22:21ff.).

This moving message, climaxed by a miraculous escape from evil, makes for a great tale of adventure and inspiration. Or it would if the implications of murderous Jews motivated by racial hatred and the implication of their rejection by God for rejecting the good news brought by Jesus did not make us squirm. To be sure, the message is clear: prophets have their fate. Jesus' career was not a series of beneficent triumphs concluded with a gruesome execution. Like other prophets, he provoked the authorities, who responded as authorities will when provoked. That fate will be shared by a prophetic church. Our problem is not simply the impetus this kind of passage has given to anti-Semitism, if this were not enough. It is that Jesus has a question to pose to us: "Who is the home team?" We must piously sit on those benches in the synagogue and righteously march to the convenient neighborhood cliff if we are to get the point. We are those who in one way or another pluck up and destroy prophets who seek to plant and build. We love them when dead, enshrining their sayings in our hearts and adorning their tombs with monuments, naming our streets in their honor and abstaining from work on the days hallowed to their memory. Living prophets are a different matter altogether.

Fifth Sunday after the Epiphany
Fifth Sunday in Ordinary Time

Lectionary	First Lesson	Psalm	Second Lesson	Gospel
Revised Common	Isa. 6:1-8, (9-13)	Psalm 138	I Cor. 15:1-11	Luke 5:1-11
Episcopal (BCP)	Judges 6:11-24a	Psalm 85 or 85:7-13	I Cor. 15:1-11	Luke 5:1-11
Roman Catholic	Isa. 6:1-8	Ps. 138:1-5, 7-8	I Cor. 15:1-11 or 15:3-8, 11	Luke 5:1-11
Lutheran (LBW)	Isa. 6:1-8, (9-13)	Ps. 85:8-13	I Cor. 14:12b-20	Luke 5:1-11

FIRST LESSON: ISAIAH 6:1-8, (9-13); JUDGES 6:11-24a

Isaiah 6:1-8, (9-13). However introduced, liturgical readings always confront hearers with a beginning. The proper place for a prophetic call, as last week's reading from Jeremiah 1 indicates, is at the beginning of the prophet's ministry. Isaiah begins *in medias res*, with five chapters of awesome oracles preceding an explanation of how this prophet came to be inspired and commissioned. The suspense this long prelude creates is something for the exegete to keep in mind, although there is suspense and mystery enough in chap. 6. The *LBW* and Revised Common Lectionaries permit the inclusion of vv. 9-13. This expansion exposes the fate of prophets: to be neglected.

"In the year that King Uzziah died" follows the convention of giving prophetic calls a specific anchor in time and space. Christian interpretation has not always been attentive to the specificity of prophetic messages, their original application to definite situations. Establishment of these situations provides historical clarity. Proclaimers cannot rest with historical information, however interesting, but awareness of that situation helps equip them in two ways: first, by asserting that the prophetic ministry speaks to concrete situations rather than to vague or timeless generalities; second, by providing checks against analogies that may be cheap or inappropriate.

To speak of the year that King Uzziah died (c. 738 B.C.E.) was also to say, in effect, "in the last of the good old days." The initial verse thus implicitly contrasts transitory mortal life and prosperity with the transcendent majesty of God. Worship provided the setting for Isaiah's call. Homilists may find it convenient to contrast worship with "real life" and Sunday piety with Monday through Saturday secularity—a problem for which church leaders must assume most of the blame, anyway—but the dichotomy between cult and genuine obedience can overlook the reality of religious life and experience. The setting of this text characterizes worship as epiphany, of which earthquake, light, and smoke are common features. (See the discussion of Isa. 60:1-6 under The Epiphany of Our Lord, above.) Isaiah's vision is prompted—which is not to say caused—by his worship experience. The "throne" is that upon which the ark sat; the altar of incense supplies the smoke and a coal for purification. The vision begins with a simple but arresting phrase: "I saw the LORD." One may hope for a detailed description, but the seer only notes the hem of God's robe. It is not likely that the prophet believed that the major, if not sole, subject of interest was the fashions then prevailing in the celestial court, however. This anthropomorphism is a synecdoche. One does not see, or need to see, God. The merest aspect of divine reality "fills the temple," exhausts the limits of human perception.

From that hem the narrator's eyes pass to the seraphim. Heavenly courts were imagined as analogies of, and thus prototypes for, earthly throne rooms. The iconographic model of angels that has fixed itself in Christian imagination and piety comes from the Greek personification of Victory. These creatures have both animal an human attributes. Six wings are not for greater speed. Two pairs cover their eyes and genitals ("feet" is a euphemism), respectively. (The Roman Catholic lectionary omits this portion.) This detail magnifies God's glory by showing that even such exalted and ever-present creatures as seraphs live in constant reverence and awe. Their acclamation is a crescendo, the repeated "Holy" evoking the superlative. "Hosts" is somewhat unclear, but probably comes from the background of "holy war," a pervasive motif of the Hebrew Bible, now troublesome to many, not just because of the image of God as warrior, but even more because of what has been done in the name of holy war: *jihads*, crusades, ethnic cleansings, witch-hunts, and inquisitions. The modern liturgical hendyadis, "God of power and might," is less colorful but does seek to preserve the positive thrust of this image. The whole passage works as a splendid commentary upon the liturgical *Sanctus*.

Isaiah's response is typical: the sight of God is disastrous for mortals. "Typical" means, or should mean, frequent. Through these words modern people, who do not expect God or angels to drop in for lunch, but who are often in danger of a casual approach to holy moments and sacred things, may be moved to rekindle their sense of awe, which is not to be confused with scrupulosity. For the clergy this loss of awe is an ever-present danger. Remember that the "original" *Sanctus* was followed by an earthquake.

"Unclean lips" turns out not to have been an inept phrase, as one of the seraphs cauterizes his mouth with a coal from the altar. This is an action of more than ritual significance. Forgiveness of sins is more than cleansing a dirty pot. The purified and absolved Isaiah no longer laments his own unworthiness. When the rhetorical question of a possible candidate arises, he has an

FIFTH SUNDAY AFTER THE EPIPHANY

answer: "Send me." Between the "Woe is me" of v. 5 and the "Send me" of v. 8 one may glimpse the meaning of conversion, forgiveness, and vocation. Verses 9-13 treat the rather disappointing result of the prophet's message. God's judgment does not stand or fall with the success of prophets commissioned to communicate it. The prophetic ministry, an element of the vocation of all Christians, is not to be measured by opinion polls. When these verses are read, there is a strong contrast between the glorious majesty of the call and the meager harvest of the mission. Come what may, God's glory abides.

Judges 6:11-24a (*BCP*). Literary criticism of Judges is difficult, not least in this section, where older, more anthropomorphic accounts coexist with subsequent and more refined traditions. This is most apparent in the varying description of the visitant as an angel or as "the LORD." The reading focuses upon the "more primitive." This has its advantages, for even those who cannot recover the "first naiveté" of the early readers can, perhaps through a "second naiveté" (Paul Ricoeur), appreciate a world in which the divine and human were not separated by vast chasms. The story of Gideon has many features of the prophetic call (see the discussion of Jer. 1:4-10, the Fourth Sunday after the Epiphany, above). As the case of Moses indicates, prophets and national heroes have much in common. The overlap helps prevent us from sterilizing prophets, isolating them from such spheres as politics.

Tension between divine and human appears in vv. 11-12. The first shows a quite amiable angel who takes rest in the shade of a tree. The second is epiphanic. The narrator preserves these polarities. There is some wisdom in such comprehensiveness. With a short adverbial clause the narrative then depicts the extent of Israel's oppression. Gideon is happily engaged in the timeless tactics of peasants who conceal their produce from rapacious armies. That peasant receives an annunciation-like greeting that ascribes to him a status at some variance with his actual condition. Not in the least abashed, Gideon replies with what is called in the technical jargon of theology a damn good question: "Why?" His feet are firmly planted in the soil of reality, and he knows his history. (His summary of God's saving deeds resonates with the creed recited by Paul in 1 Corinthians 15.) What is the use of all those Bible stories recounting God's mighty acts of old except to make us even more angry and miserable? Self-fulfillment is not Gideon's aim, for he has shifted the object of the preposition from the singular to the plural. At this rather embarrassing moment, when an angel might well have served to take the heat, the (older) narrative of v. 14 reveals that his dialogue partner is God, who does not argue theodicy, but then and there commissions Gideon to straighten up the mess. If you're not part of the solution, you're part of the problem. A quite unconvinced

Gideon retorts with something like the typical prophetic objection: he and his clan stand at the bottom of the social ladder. The answer is neither complicated nor original; it is the same as v. 12: the LORD is with them. Insignificant Gideon and his paltry clan are not alone. *Dominus vobiscum* is the refrain of this passage, promise and empowerment. Even the most humble are of high status when they belong to the household of God. Proof Gideon wants, and a sign he will receive. After the word comes a meal. Gideon provides the food; the angel prepares it with a fiery touch evocative of the prophetic calls (Jer. 1:4-10; Isa. 6:1-8). Now assured that he has witnessed an epiphany, Gideon expresses the usual reservations. The divine voice brings assurance, nicely bracketing the passage that had opened with a greeting. Gideon's response? Worship. Theological reflection has transformed a meal to be shared (cf. Gen. 18:3-8) into a sacrifice of communion. The call of Gideon may be read as a parable of Christian life. Vocation comes in the midst of daily life and work, comes to those burdened by their own failures and alienated from a God they regard as impotent or inattentive. To such persons, people like us, God does not say, "Relax. I'll take care of it," but "Get going. I commission you." In response they worship and then *do* get to work, nourished by the sacrifice of thanksgiving and imbued with the peace of God that passes all understanding.

SECOND LESSON: I CORINTHIANS 15:1-11

1 Corinthians 15 provides the epistle lessons for the residue of "green" Sundays. The theme is resurrection, which was not selected as appropriate material for a final chapter, as if the apostle were producing a textbook on dogmatics. This is the last chapter of a mystery (v. 51), the climax and key to the entire document. The solution is revealed in the beginning: Christ is risen, but there is more to come and much to understand. Chapter 15 is a carefully structured rhetorical composition. Paul is certainly dealing with issues raised at Corinth, but he has chosen the order in which he will respond, and, as always, he will utilize these immediate particulars to construct arguments of general applicability. The apostle is not attempting to "prove" the resurrection of Christ, nor is he conveying new information. The "reminder" language of v. 1 serves to reassure the believers that they have the tools to answer their questions. The tool in question is the creed, which is both "text" and response, sermon and "doxology." Salvation is not static but, according to v. 2, progressive and contingent. Paul is wont to use such language in the face of those who are too confident about God's fondness for them. The creed of vv. 3-5 has two sections, each with a primary verb ("died," "rose") and a secondary verb ("buried," "appeared"). The primary verb in each case has two qualifying phrases. Of those two operative

verbs, the first, "died," would be rather unremarkable were it not for the explication: "for our sins." That was the coal of purification. The second, "rose," is the basis for getting up and going to work. Both death and resurrection conform to the promises of God ("scriptures"). All this is mediated by tradition, the laboratory of faith. The list of witnesses in v. 5 is of great interest to those engaged in exploring the movements and controversies among early Christians. In this liturgical context, as at Easter, its primary function is to place the believers upon the "foundation of apostles." This is to say that the list is not evidential but foundational.

For Paul resurrection appearances are complete. He does not envision that this list will expand. The apostles have, like Isaiah (or Gideon), been equipped for their task. The list that will grow is the baptismal register kept in heaven, as it were. In this creed all the apostles, whatever their disagreements, and all the faithful, diverse as they are, share. Why does he begin with this creed? The rest of the chapter will answer the question. In essence, the basic principle is that believers share the redeemer's fate. What happened to Jesus will happen to us. This is the ground and content of vocation. An implication of this principle is that creeds do not serve to define, and thus limit, God. They rather define us and our place in God's sight. Through reciting them we learn who we are. For this reason creeds serve as hymns of praise.

(For 1 Corinthians 14:12b-20 see the Fourth Sunday after the Epiphany.)

GOSPEL: LUKE 5:1-11

After this pericope the lectionaries will leap to the sermon of 6:17-49. As in the case of the early church of Acts 1–2, Luke portrays Jesus as meeting initial success in an atmosphere free of conflict. Although strife soon emerges, this section interweaves and thus correlates vocation and healing, with calls in 5:1-11, 27-39, healings in 5:17-26; 6:6-11, and both in the summary of 6:12-19. Reflection upon this contiguity of discipleship and health, healing and ministry, might produce some small reward. Luke has fashioned a more historically and psychologically appropriate picture of the call than did Mark (1:16-20), placing this act after a period of preaching and healing (chap. 4). The setting Luke provides shows theological reflection upon this apostolic call. To endow this event with suitable narrative coloring Luke blended into Mark an "old" account of a resurrection appearance (cf. 1 Cor. 15:1-11) in Galilee, traces of which may also be found in John 21:1-14. As a result there are literary problems to entertain carping critics.

Be this as it may and is, the results are worth any flaws. The opening displays Jesus' great success. Casting about for a solution to the problem this has caused, he sees two boats, whose occupants were not "pressing in to hear the word of God." "Washing their nets" encapsulates their long labor of nocturnal fishing. For all the readers know, this was the best night they ever had. Jesus commandeers one of these boats, the owner of which was a certain Simon. Of the teaching that followed we hear nothing. Class over, Jesus turns his mind to the fishing business. Like Gideon and the prophets, Simon is skeptical. Why follow a long and fruitless night with a daytime effort, plagued by heat and inferior circumstances? "Yet, if you say so. . . ." This Simon has taken some notice of an authority who can not only take over his boat but also tell him how to do his job. And rightly so, for the product exceeded their capacity. The ubiquitous and mysterious "they" of vv. 6-7 are fully attentive to business. Even two boats are not enough. The largest catch in recorded history will do no good at the bottom of the lake. Simon Peter, as he is now called, has a different reaction. Like Isaiah (6:5), he recognizes the manifestation of divine glory and its threat. This water is not safe for sinners to swim in. After the others have been awkwardly incorporated, Jesus makes his famous invitation, followed by an equally famous response. The biggest catch in history lies rotting in abandoned boats on the beach.

By translating the mysterious call of Mark 1:16-20 into a miraculous epiphany of an objective type Peter's call acquires some of the characteristics of Paul's (Acts 9). Yet this is more than elegant parallelism or a vivid introduction to the ministry of Peter. Resurrection faith (1 Cor. 15:1-11) is the basis for both the gospel and the Gospels. The Christ who calls is the one proclaimed in the mission of the church. Conversion and vocation are the fundamental miracles. Assimilation of the calls of Peter (and Paul) to those of prophets is patent. The leading disciples of Jesus were not called while engaged in a religious quest (the only example of this was a failure, Mark 10:17-31), or even, like Isaiah, "in church," but, like Gideon, in the midst of their daily life and work. They were also called "from." At the beginning of this story Peter is an apparently successful professional. At the end he has become an amateur. Thus it is with the Christian vocation.

The announcement of his forgiveness takes the form of a new job description. In these phrases Luke, like the prophetic writers, depicts absolution not as a state but as empowerment. Vocation includes renunciation, giving up all. Wealth is for Luke both real and symbolic. In return there will be new kinds of wealth. Fish? This is not a metaphor to overdo, for it has connotations of entrapment and consumption. In the background are prophetic (Jeremiah 16) and parabolic images of judgment. Hooking fish and reeling them in does not intimate evangelism and ministry of the kinder and gentler sort. Rather than stress fishing I suggest attention to v. 4. This is what vocation so often requires, going out further and casting deeper, stretching ourselves because this is what the Master of Peter, you, and me has invited us to do in quest of the best catch in history, recorded or not.

Sixth Sunday after the Epiphany
Sixth Sunday in Ordinary Time/Proper 1

Lectionary	First Lesson	Psalm	Second Lesson	Gospel
Revised Common	Jer. 17:5-10	Psalm 1	1 Cor. 15:12-20	Luke 6:17-26
Episcopal (BCP)	Jer. 17:5-10	Psalm 1	1 Cor. 15:12-20	Luke 6:17-26
Roman Catholic	Jer. 17:5-8	Ps. 1:1-4, 6	1 Cor. 15:12, 16-20	Luke 6:17, 20-26
Lutheran (LBW)	Jer. 17:5-8	Psalm 1	1 Cor. 15:12, 16-20	Luke 6:17-26

FIRST LESSON: JEREMIAH 17:5-10

The lectionary's intention in selecting this passage is clear: a corollary with the series of blessings and curses that opens the Sermon on the Plain. One can find more here than "Old Testament" parallels. The similes begun in vv. 6 and 8 are an effective condensation of the entire sermon, which ends with a parable contrasting two types of hearers (Luke 6:48-49). This frame is all the more useful in that there are rarely enough Sundays after Epiphany to complete the reading of the Sermon.

This section of Jeremiah is a bit of a jumble and includes material of dubious authenticity, some of which is wisdom rather than prophecy. There are two clear units: vv. 5-8, which set forth in antithetical form and subsequent illustration the cursed and the blessed, and vv. 9-10, a proverb with theological interpretation. The first unit has many parallels, notably Psalm 1. In the background is the arid climate of the Near East, where water supply was a problem. The same image drives the initial parable of Jesus (Mark 4:1-8 and parallels). Survival requires deep roots. The wisdom tradition often deals with motivation. From this Jeremiah could relate the Torah and its covenant to interiority, specifically the heart. What are, to employ the same metaphor, the grounds for self-understanding? That which is grounded in itself has no roots and cannot acquire nourishment in "dry" times. The words may be old, but few could be more relevant to contemporary North American culture, probably the world's most individualistic. Our individualism reflects that freedom which we properly cherish. To us, cultures based upon community norms seem repressive. Since the various social worlds of the Bible, despite their diversities, are essentially group-oriented, reading the Bible is always a countercultural experience for us. Like the Sermon on the Plain, this passage is less a blast against "secular humanism" than a critique of any subjectivity that deceives itself by presuming to be objective.

The added saying in vv. 9-10 reinforces the point. Sages regarded the "heart" as unfathomable. In contemporary terms we should say that humans cannot analyze themselves because the observer and the observed are one and the same. The writer appends a theological conclusion: What is opaque to mortals is transparent to God, whose judgments stand. If those judgments often seem no more fathomable than the human heart, this says more about human limitations than about divine caprice. Beatitude, the state extolled in the Sermon, begins and ends with reliance upon God as both source and norm of justice. As in all sapiential constructs, there are dangers. "Act–consequence" remains popular. Those who touch the stove burn their fingers. Act–consequence is obviously no more than a *model*. Not every speeder is caught. Jeremiah sagely seeks, in taking up the ideas of the sages, both to relate act to consequence and to avoid human desires to lock up God in a deterministic system. God remains free to execute justice, of which God alone is judge. What seems at the time to be a blessing may in the long run look more like a curse.

SECOND LESSON: I CORINTHIANS 15:12-20

(For a general introduction, see the comments on 1 Cor. 15:1-11 for the Fifth Sunday after the Epiphany.) Only in v. 12 does Paul come to the "problem." Although the phrase "no resurrection of the dead" seems clear, the precise nature of this hypothetical assertion is not certain, and Paul himself may not have been fully aware of the issue, as his source may have been unclear. For Paul, resurrection is an apocalyptic promise for believers whose existence is shaped by the resurrection of Christ, itself an apocalyptic event. Apocalyptic was no easier to communicate then than it is now. Apocalyptic events are not "historical"; they are not accessible to human witnesses. The resurrection of Jesus was not the resuscitation of a corpse, as it were, to a prolonged mode of earthly existence, but the translation of Christ into the eschatological realm. As an apocalyptic event resurrection is neither a bit of historical good fortune experienced by Jesus, as if it were the reward due a hero for great achievements, nor a spiritual experience enjoyed by the baptized, as in, for example, the discovery through initiation or revelation of one's immortal soul.

Bodily resurrection was neither a popular nor a readily intelligible concept for most ancients, who were likely to view it as impossible and undesirable. Immortality appealed to those who lived by and for their minds, for whom loss of consciousness was (and is) the greatest of tragedies. The wealthy and powerful, well rewarded in this life, had little need for an afterlife. Bodily resurrection emerges historically in the context of martyrdom (Dan. 12:1-3) and socially among those lives were determined by what their bodies could accomplish. Paul was charged with universalizing a notion that, it might be said, would have appealed to peasants and soldiers, but not to sages or rulers. For him bodily resurrection became the medium for arguing a continuity not based upon the satisfaction of differing individual aspirations. Resurrection of the body will be the perfection of the body of Christ.

One likely understanding is that those who said there is no resurrection viewed themselves as already able to get "out of the body" through spiritual experiences (chaps. 12–13) and who therefore looked forward only to the final and permanent dissolution of body and soul. What is less likely is that there were some skeptics who regarded resurrection as "scientifically impossible." After grounding his thesis in the communal creed (vv. 1-11), Paul takes up one of its implications. The creed, to reiterate, is not just a story about God, but also a part of our story. In religiohistorical language one says that the redeemer and redeemed share the same fate. This is what drives Paul's case: those denying the resurrection isolate Christ from the believers. Through Christ's death and resurrection believers have been empowered with forgiveness of sins (v. 17). His vindication was not escape from the body but the inauguration of a new age. Resurrection is not mere "fact." It is power. Hope is oriented to and impelled by the other world, not the limits of "this life" (v. 19).

Verse 20 forms an inclusion with v. 12. Within its frame Paul has sought to establish the meaning of Christ's resurrection as the signal of a new age. Denial of resurrection fractures the body by separating the living from the dead. In the language of the Apostles' Creed the departed would be ousted from the "communion of saints" and the "holy catholic church" would become no more than an association. Verse 20 introduces another religiohistorical image: "first fruits." All sacrifices are synecdoches, parts affirming that the whole comes from God. Ancients routinely offered the gods their initial returns of plants, animals, and sometimes children, as a means to assure continued harvest. Through this agricultural trope, Paul asserts that the raising of Christ is the part that determines and guarantees the resurrection of the entire *Corpus Christi*.

So what does all of this have to do with us? We want to reap the harvests of our software and gather the fruits of the Internet without reading those manuals. Strange as it may sound, these words speak to those of us, including parts and moments of each of us, that would like to begin the creed with the resurrection (start off on a positive note), omitting the crucifixion. "Saying there is no resurrection" is an attempt to distinguish our lives from that of Jesus. One—not the only—impulse behind the current "historical Jesus" research is a desire to find a Jesus unencumbered by the Christ of creeds, a Jesus without myth. For such endeavors Paul is always a nuisance, because for him the myth is all that really matters. The tag "no cross, no crown" is trite, but it is an alliterative handle to Paul and for Paul, who used it to dig deeply into that well of life from which living waters flow.

GOSPEL: LUKE 6:17-26

The Gospels for the remaining Sundays of Ordinary Time present the Lukan Sermon on the Plain (hereafter Sermon). Luke's stories are famous, but in the case of the Sermon Matthew has won in a walk. The principle underlying the three-year lectionary is not simply to edify the faithful with more biblical texts but to allow each Synoptic Gospel to have its day, even if history has left it for the dogs. The very dogs get crumbs, and there is a particle or two of value in this Sermon. Those who like things light will note that Luke does it in twenty-nine verses, while Matthew consumes one hundred and eleven. Yet this is far from "lite" ethics, not least in its opening. Our major problem is not that we must this year deal with the Brand X of Gospel sermons, but the way in which that Sermon is perceived. This Sermon, aided by misperceptions of the Sermon on the Mount, strikes our ears as a list of rules and demands, virtues to be adopted, "morality" of the "You'd better watch out; you'd better not pout" sort. The Sermon does not work by oracles or legal pronouncements but through rhetoric. It is an organized attempt to persuade people to see things in a new way. Some of these rhetorical tactics, including initial shock, are apparent enough. Others lurk in the Greek original or in techniques no longer in favor. The goal of this rhetorical effort is not to resolve problems by bringing reflection to an end with a ready supply of ultimate answers but to get people to *think*. Overcoming this pervasive heresy is one of the leading challenges to those who would proclaim the Sermons on the Mount or the Plain. Dated as it is, the contents and structure offer some hints at how this may be done. Note the resonance between beginning and end, the frequent appeals to common sense, and, above all, the abundance and vividness of the images. There is some wisdom here.

Wisdom, including proverbs, supplies much of the content. The structure of the speech invites comparison with the speeches of "Dame Wisdom," the personified figure of Proverbs chaps. 1 and 8; Sirach 24; and so forth, who offers her hearers two choices, with promises for those who select wisdom and threats for those who do not. A danger of the "two ways" model, already raised in the reading from Jeremiah, is the "either-or" demand, the limits of which are enhanced by the perception that the fix is in. Who would choose folly? This is, of course, the very object of the Sermon, to lead people to start out on the right path. Much of its wisdom resembles nothing so much as folly, a theme developed in a different way by Paul (1 Corinthians 1–4). This is wisdom in a new key.

The context is not unimportant. The Sermon follows a mountaintop experience, to which Jesus had withdrawn for a long prayer vigil, following which he chose twelve apostles. Then he descends to the plain, to be received by a crowd that has come from all Palestine, including its Gentile fringes, come to hear and be healed. This solemn prelude reiterates the unity and miraculous character of word and deed. The following brief remarks are not directed at this diverse crowd but "his disciples." Quite innocent of subsequent advances in homiletics, Jesus does not begin with a few jokes to loosen people up or with a story about his own experiences. Instead he opens by dropping a series of bombs, the explosions of which have not yet ceased to reverberate.

Beatitudes are difficult. Scholars will say that the form is sapiential. Macarisms of the wisdom schools describe the wise and thus both how to be wise and the rewards of wisdom. These do not conform to that tradition. Form and content clash in unpleasant tension. The beatitudes turn pigs' ears into silk purses. By ancient standards these are antibeatitudes and counterwoes. Christians have therefore tended to read them, if they are theologically inclined, as conditions of salvation, or, if behavior is their interest, as a list of virtues. The difficulty with these related approaches is less that they are not especially attractive selling points than that, when all is said and done, it is not particularly difficult to get oneself into the position of being poor, hungry, unhappy, and persecuted. The Jesus of Luke is not suggesting that only adolescents belong to the kingdom of God. What, then, are these weird benedictions? They are nothing more and nothing less than announcements of salvation (cf. Luke 4:18-19; Jesus, it would appear, had but one sermon). If this is true, God's standards may not precisely coincide with ours in every particular. Since, by God's standards, none merit salvation, salvation begins with the understanding that the world has been turned upside down and inside out. The beatitudes proclaim that things are neither what they seem to be nor fair. This is bad news to rich and poor alike, for all want things to be fair for us and reality and appearance to diverge when this variance is flattering. In one sense every beatitude says the same thing, confirmed by each corresponding woe. The list could be extended indefinitely, but the point would not change.

From another angle each beatitude is an inexhaustible resource. The object of the first is "the poor," the most general category and the only group for whom the explanatory clause is in the present tense. In obvious contrast with Matt. 5:3, Luke does not spiritualize the poor. This is a social group, encompassing all whom we call "the marginalized." Pushed to the margins of Caesar's empire, they belong to God's kingdom. This is not to say that they own that kingdom or rule it (cf. 22:29), but that God accepts those whom others reject. The three following macarisms provide specific examples of marginalization, contrasting present to future, but governed by the present of v. 20 to exclude the notion that all blessings relate to a coming payday in the sky. These cover the physical, emotional/spiritual, and social realms, each of which is distinct but none of which may be isolated. The final beatitude (vv. 22-23) is the most developed and also the most credal and ecclesiological, climaxing the series with the understanding that happiness belongs to those who accept the call of God. This accords with the prophetic and vocational themes of the preceding Sundays. Only here is there an imperative, "Rejoice and leap for joy." The future in which the tears of v. 21b will turn to laughter is the time of persecution. Yet even this present joy is based upon the futurity of recompense. Salvation is both present and future, present in that God is not simply waiting with infinite patience to even up the score, future in that no human longings or desires can comprehend it. The woe to the rich does not precede an affirmation of future poverty. They have sufficient consolation (cf. Luke 16:19-31). Reversals are in store for those who believe that their present happiness will never end and are confident that high standing in public opinion polls is proof of their virtue. (The NRSV obscures an important distinction between beatitudes and woes. With the exception of the final blessing, the beatitudes are general: *the* poor, *the* hungry, *the* mourners, whereas the woes are direct: *you* rich, *you* who laugh, *you* in good repute.)

The two central Lukan beatitudes make an explicit contrast between "now" and the future. These seek to lead all to reflect on, as we say, "where they are now." Now can be the time of salvation or the opportunity for overlooking the call for repentance and change. The Gospel as a whole, in particular its parables, warns against viewing now as either judgment or grace, of assuming that God does not like me or that I am among God's favored ones. The beatitudes surely shock in their claim that God is different. They also invite self-examination and reflection, assessment and renewal. The announcement that things will never be the same again *is* an announcement of salvation because it puts forth the possibility of grace.

So, to those who would see in the beatitudes a thin and unappetizing diet, say that this is a feeding miracle, bread of life and cup of redemption. Luke provides two allusions: in v. 17 Jesus (1) raises his eyes, as he will do at 9:16, before multiplying the loaves, a feast at which (2) all ate to their heart's content, precisely (in Greek) as the hungry of 6:21 were promised. In the eucharist the poor enter God's kingdom, the hungry are fed, mourners consoled, and outcasts included. And what if, in the aftermath and after mass, none of this is continued? Jesus and Luke answer that in a single short word: woe.

Seventh Sunday after the Epiphany
Seventh Sunday in Ordinary Time/Proper 2

Lectionary	First Lesson	Psalm	Second Lesson	Gospel
Revised Common	Gen. 45:3-11, 15	Ps. 37:1-11, 39-40	I Cor. 15:35-38, 42-50	Luke 6:27-38
Episcopal (BCP)	Gen. 45:3-11, 21-28	Ps. 37:1-18 or 37:3-10	I Cor. 15:35-38, 42-50	Luke 6:27-38
Roman Catholic	I Sam. 26:2, 7-9, 12-13, 22-23	Ps. 103:1-4, 8, 10, 12-13	I Cor. 15:45-49	Luke 6:27-38
Lutheran (LBW)	Gen. 45:3-8a, 15	Ps. 103:1-13	I Cor. 15:35-38a, 42-50	Luke 6:27-38

FIRST LESSON: GENESIS 45:3-11, 15, 21-28; I SAMUEL 26:2, 7-9, 12-13, 22-23

Genesis 45:3-11, 15, 21-28 (*LBW/BCP*/Revised Common). This great scene of recognition acquires its lectionary place here as a narrative example of doing good to one's enemies. The recognition, as in a number of resurrection stories, is also a revelation. The account should be savored, with awareness that its sentimental appeal is in danger of clouding the renunciation of revenge. It might not be a bad idea for the lector concisely to summarize the story of Joseph, from nomadic prosperity to rather less than rags, followed by an astonishing rise to dizzying heights. A somewhat similar story is told about Jesus in Phil. 2:6-11.

Joseph's first announcement is a bit of a flop. He is willing to walk the extra mile. Drawing the group to him, he assures them that what humans do for wicked ends is not always the end, for God can fashion great things from our evil motives and shallow deeds. This is what providence means, that even within the worst situations there are redemptive possibilities, for both malefactor and victims. The moment of greatest shame or ultimate despair can yet be an opportunity for grace. These are gracious words, but they can easily be misused, as my comments on the Gospel seek to indicate. Joseph is not, after all, speaking as a condemned slave who nonetheless assigns his misfortune to the will of God. He can forgive because he has been vindicated and holds the power to build up or to destroy. Abstention from vengeance presupposes the power to wreak vengeance. One cannot use this story to exhort victims of abuse to accept their status or to excuse those who will abuse again. Joseph does not say, "You guys are really bad, but I'm going to let you off the hook this time." His own success in Egypt leads him to the interpretation that God's mysterious hand has been at work. This interpretation offers the possibility of reconciliation.

The *BCP* lectionary's inclusion of vv. 21-28 rounds the account off. This is a resurrection story. Who has been raised? Joseph, his brothers, and his father, raised by grace that changed and renewed each and all of them.

1 Samuel 26:2, 7-9, 12-13, 22-23 (Roman Catholic). This reading, like that from Genesis used in the other lectionaries, is a narrative example of doing good to those who hate you. The example is another prototype of Jesus: David the king. Saul was bent upon putting David to death. On two occasions (chap. 24 being the former) David refused to slay his persecutor. When David learns of the arrival of Saul's army, he proposes a clandestine mission. Abishai, the brother of Joab, agrees to accompany him into the nerve center of the enemy's camp: the tent of the king (cf. the story of Judith). Abishai makes the obvious proposal: assassinate Saul with his own spear. God has placed him in our hands. David piously declines. The matter should be left in God's hands. Instead they remove the water jar and spear as proof that "Kilroy was here." They could scarcely have pulled off this outrageous stunt had the Lord not intervened. Verses 22-23 report the subsequent encounter in which David graciously returns the sword and explains his refusal to exploit the situation.

Outside of the specific motive, the sacred cnaracter of monarchs, which is not a current issue in North American society, the passage has some useful points. Beyond the refusal to execute justice, to kill one seeking to kill you, there emerges the question of just what providence is and means. Abishai is certain: Who can turn down such a God-given opportunity? David's own interpretation, which comes, unfortunately, in v. 10, is that if God wishes Saul dead, God will see that this happens. Cheap interpretations of providence, whether negative—"God does not like me"—or positive—"This opportunity must come from God"—are often made in the service of one's self. Providence is not about a master switchboard operator who passes the time by giving opportunities to one person and blows to another. In fact, providence is the very opposite of taking the matter into one's own hands. These views inform and enlarge the Sermon's injunctions against retaliation. Not all will agree with David, of course. Among them were the servants of another emperor. When they take it upon themselves to lay hands upon one they ironically acclaim as "King of the Jews" the spear and the water bucket will be available to serve their needs.

SECOND LESSON: I CORINTHIANS 15:35-50

Although the several authorities abbreviate this section in different ways, proclaimers will benefit from reflection upon the entire unit and its context. In the omitted vv. 21-34 Paul has introduced a variant of the "apocalyptic

SEVENTH SUNDAY AFTER THE EPIPHANY

timetable," not as the ever-popular means for calculating the end, but as a pointer to show where we are. The amply-proportioned soprano has not offered her final aria. Some of those at Corinth have begun their applause a bit prematurely. Verses 35 and following utilize one of these celebrants' more popular types of composition, wisdom speculation, and do so in the fashion of popular education (diatribe), with its hypothetical questions, brisk phrases, and analogies from science, nature, and everyday life.

The apostle does not have a "crudely materialistic" view of resurrection. The challenge he faces is to argue for a continuity between the earthly and heavenly bodies that will not imply that the heavenly body will be composed of an earthly substance, on the one hand, while, on the other hand, contending against the kind of discontinuity—implied, for example, in soul-body dualism—that would undergird claims that what is done with our earthly bodies and in the terrestrial body of Christ is irrelevant. He begins with an analogy from planting. Seeds are "buried" in the ground, "die," in order that they may produce plants. All lectionaries take a pass on vv. 38b-41 because they use now confusing concepts from outmoded science. Verses 42-44 build, by means of an almost hypnotic rhythm and rhyme ("sown . . . raised" rhyme in Greek) a contrast between the pre- and postresurrection states, to the advantage in the latter. At its climax comes a daring oxymoron: a "spiritual body," contrasted to the "physical" (literally "psychic") body. For proof of this bold proposal Paul offers Gen. 2:7, one of the most discussed and controverted passages in early Christianity. In Greek it says that the first man became a "living *psyche*." Paul's argument is both clear and revolutionary. Rather than the common notion of a preexistent spiritual element (soul) injected into physical matter, he establishes the order (*a*) physical and (*b*) spiritual. In contrast to the first Adam the second will be a "life-giving *pneuma*." Genuine pneumatic existence, even possession of the divine image, belongs to the future. The conclusion in v. 50, a source of enormous difficulty for patristic exegetes, sounds dualistic. His object is less speculation about heavenly existence than assertion that what we have now is not permanent, including our spiritual gifts.

Heavy going, by any lights. What are church leaders to do with this passage? Most will not discuss it, quite properly driven by the centrality of the Gospel, but some explanation seems to be needed. Here is Paul the theologian, spewing forth complex anthropology. The pessimistic anthropology here implied became characteristic of Western Christianity, through the heritage of Augustinianism. In due course it would be said that humans had, in the fall, lost the divine image. Paul actually implies that we never had it, however *ad hoc* his reasoning. Nowhere is the dividing line between classic Eastern and classic Western Christianity clearer. Perhaps the most radical element of Paul's thesis is one implicit in the stories of Joseph and David and explicit in Luke 4:16-30 (the Gospel for the Third and Fourth Sundays after the Epiphany): you can't go home again. Ancient society, and nearly all societies until the Enlightenment, saw the Golden Age as belonging to the past and the goal as returning to the good old days when Adam had no need to plow nor Eve to weave. The Christian Bible begins in a garden and ends in a city.

This passage exposes Paul as a thorn in our flesh. Why does he not just tell "those people" to shut up, or to abandon the pursuit of wisdom, and so forth? Why must he seek to use theology to make a fairly clear pastoral case? If an editorial comment is appropriate, I say "Thank God for Paul," who realized that there is always some theological rationale present and sought to talk not only about practice but also why. One presumed characteristic of Americans is that we always ask why something is or is to be done. From this angle the apostle is 100 percent American.

GOSPEL: LUKE 6:27-38

This section of the Sermon has a clear theme, discussion of act-consequence from the perspectives of reciprocity and retaliation. The idea of conforming one's behavior to the expected reactions of others is not alien to us, but two related dimensions of ancient Mediterranean social life help clarify the original impact of these verses: reciprocity and honor/shame. Maintenance of honor, a social currency of nearly fixed supply, and avoidance of shame were collective responsibilities. One who struck you on the cheek had shamed your entire family, or, if a "foreigner," your whole village. Ancient reciprocity was socially graded, with those at the top serving as benefactors who were to use their wealth, extracted from the poor, for the public good. The less advantaged were, in turn, to repay this benefaction by returning honor to their betters. The economy was not viewed as an entity capable of unlimited growth but as a pie of enduring size. If I receive a large slice, someone else will get very little, or nothing. Like New England villagers who do not wish to be "beholden" to others, recipients of favors strove to return them as soon as conveniently possible. The sermon both assumes and challenges these implicit understandings and values.

Structurally this section has four units, united by form and subject. The rhetoric is important. If all Jesus wished to say was "do not retaliate," that he could have said. Whether or not this is a good idea, few will embrace it because of a simple admonition. Verses 27-30 are a crescendo of short, snappy, countercultural commands, beginning with the most general and concluding with the most comprehensive. These commands are less than literal and more than figurative. Like the beatitudes they could be expanded indefinitely. What is supplied is enough to show that the field is not narrow but also not so detailed as to weary. The first words slip quickly by—too quickly. "But" implies an adversative. Unlike the Sermon on the Mount, where such adversatives follow a Bible verse, the antecedent here is honor given to false prophets and the shame heaped upon true prophets. "To you that listen"—"listen" is a rather important verb in Luke. This is a good time to consult that concordance.

Loving enemies brings no honor and achieves no reciprocity. As in the beatitudes, ordinary wisdom and normal values are being turned upside down. Under the crushing weight of tradition these words come as invitations to passivity and thus invitations to that passive-aggressive life that afflicts believers more than others. In view here is not passivity but power, power no less available to the weak than to the strong. Through shock Jesus invites us not to accept violence and abuse as our proper due, but to do something about it. Those who strike back may find themselves in an uneven conflict with someone who can strike harder. They have already lost in that they have allowed their adversary to set the terms of the conflict. Nonviolence is a form of birth control designed to prevent violence from begetting violence. Its object is not crushing one's enemy but changing enemies into friends. Mahatma Gandhi and Martin Luther King Jr. correctly understood the message of the Sermon as the proclamation of a new kind of power rather than as an exhortation for believers to be Satan's punching bags.

Verse 31 is a pivot between the opening section on nonretaliation and the following exposure of most love as self-service, vv. 32-34, itself a continuation of the theme of v. 27. The "Golden Rule" is both a commonplace and an inadequate summary of the ethics of Jesus or of Christian ethics. When isolated, as it most often is, the rule is rather narcissistic, not simply anthropocentric, or even egocentric, for it presumes that what I want is what others also desire. Through its strict construction I should give my wife a fine and complete set of the Teubner edition of Plutarch for Christmas, and she should give me a pair of earrings. If we do not so understand the rule, it is because we have listened to this sermon, which pushes us to a new understanding: "Do unto others as God, who is merciful, would do." A venerable tradition of exegesis notes that the rule occurs in Jewish texts, but in negative form, which is judged to be inferior. This is erroneous, since ancient Christian texts also give the negative form. This judgment may also reveal, to those in search of the same, a certain irony, for it violates the Golden Rule. Interpret the texts and beliefs of other movements as you would have them interpret those of your own group.

Verses 32-34 speak of actions based upon the predictability of gain. These have nothing to do with "love." Examples include the love given by parents to children, teachers to students, clergy to their parishioners. When one views this as a "loan" to be repaid, possibly with interest, the result is a closed circle, not unlike the circle of violence. Such love is given so that the recipients will, in turn, share it with others. We are children ourselves, children of God who have received vast amounts of love to share. God is the ultimate model, and God is merciful even to those who show no recognition. This notion of the imitation of God is one of the ways in which the Sermon manifests a confident anthropology. This has, in turn, made it a burden to those who approach it as weak and guilty sinners, for whom it will seem an incitement to greater guilt and thus to moral paralysis. One path out of this cycle of guilt is to understand that for Christians the Sermon is about grace, about the possibility of new life, about what those adopted as sons and daughters of the Most High can discover as possibilities rather than as judgments.

This capacity for mercy both derives from and issues in leaving judgment to God (vv. 37-38). This is less self-denial than it is freedom. The freedom not to have to strike back, not to need to measure tit for tat, not to spend one's time issuing rulings from the bench of justice, is what this Sermon is all about. There are commands in abundance here, mostly commands to let go and be free, and there are promises as well, promises of reward and return, neither of which is postponed to the afterlife. These rewards include but are not limited to the reward of not letting others set the rules for conflict or not having to calculate what one will get back. God has changed the rules so that mortals may be free to worship God and love others. This is what Joseph, David, Paul, and Jesus have to say today. It is also what the worshiping community acts out every week. God, too, has but a single sermon.

Eighth Sunday after the Epiphany
Eighth Sunday in Ordinary Time/Proper 3

Lectionary	First Lesson	Psalm	Second Lesson	Gospel
Revised Common	Sir. 27:4-7 or Isa. 55:10-13	Ps. 92:1-4, 12-15	1 Cor. 15:51-58	Luke 6:39-49
Episcopal (BCP)	Jer. 7:1-7, (8-15)	Psalm 92 or 92:1-5, 11-14	1 Cor. 15:50-58	Luke 6:39-49
Roman Catholic	Sir. 27:4-7	Ps. 92:2-3, 13-16	1 Cor. 15:54-58	Luke 6:39-45
Lutheran (LBW)	Jer. 7:1-7, (8-15)	Psalm 92	1 Cor. 15:51-58	Luke 6:39-49

FIRST LESSON: JEREMIAH 7:1-7, (8-15); SIRACH 27:4-7

Jeremiah 7:1-7, (8-15) (*LBW/BCP*). Jeremiah's famous "temple sermon" resonates with the parable that closes today's Gospel, both in image ("house") and in theme (security). Jeremiah 26:1-9, the parallel, gives a more detailed description of the setting. The date was c. 609 B.C.E., the occasion a holiday service. It is not surprising that the festive crowd did not receive Jeremiah's message with unbounded appreciation or that, like Jesus, he would eventually be mobbed by the crowd and come to the attention of the police. The minds of the worshipers were on other things. In that regard, and only in that regard, they have something in common with God. Otherwise the Almighty is displeased enough to order Jeremiah to disrupt the sacred festivities. This honor God needs no more than any other. The message appears to be that of an anticultic ethical reformer, an enthusiast for right rather than rite. The reformation had already taken place, however, under Josiah, and the issues related more to what was done outside of "church" rather than in it. To be sure, the people had come to view the temple as a talisman and "This is the temple of the LORD" as a charm against misfortune. Behind this was more than superstition, of which there was certainly enough. The people had perverted the covenant by viewing it as a one-way street, an unconditional promise by God on their behalf. Rather than seeing worship as an instrument of this covenant, they took the more pleasing view that it was a blanket promise of magical protection. Having God's word, they would hold God responsible. Things do not work quite that way. God served as the Lord and protector precisely in order to provide justice. Verse 6 places true worship and just conduct on the same level. Jeremiah was interested in liturgy in all its ramifications, cultic, social, and theological. Through v. 7 there is no threat, only promise, promise coupled with a request: "Let me dwell with you in this place." They had the temple, but it was an inn without room for God.

Grace is not cheap, a predicate that also applies to sermons. One can easily, with the help of oracles from on high and the hindsight of history, see the point and miss the target. Nations, religious bodies, and individuals are bereft neither of a sense of entitlement, nor of accusing others of breaking promises when we do not keep our side of the bargain. The life of faith is not a bargain purchase of immunity. Some of the greatest hindrances to life together are the deeds of entitlement, often implicit, that we carry about as we collect grievances and engage in jeremiads against those who wrong us. Such entitlements are beams of wood in our eyes. The entitlements of others may be mere specks, but we are not hesitant to point them out as obstacles that would best be removed. All this, prophets would tell us, is eyewash.

Sirach 27:4-7 (Roman Catholic/Revised Common). Sages were careful observers of life, in which the wise could discern the structure of the world. Words being their business, sages found them of particular interest. In an obvious corollary to the forthcoming passage from the Sermon on the Plain, Ben Sira presents a series of three succinct comparisons from work life to make his point. These repetitions provide both a cumulative and an inclusive case. If one image does not strike home, another will. The whole world makes the same point. Although proverbial, each image has found a place in the prophetic tradition, and all of them have been touched upon in the readings for these Sundays. They are images of judgment, the God who sifts wheat, shatters worthless pots, and has fruitless trees chopped down and burned. Wisdom did not reject the judgment of God, but it also affirmed, as do Jesus and Paul, that human beings serve as their own judges.

Judgment is also revelation, exposure. When we become too worried about what God is doing or not doing to straighten up one mess or another, the time is ripe for us to be shown that we are judging ourselves by presuming to judge God or others. Discretion and custody of the tongue have their merits, but they, too, are forms of speech and judgment. What are we saying if we can offer no more than "This is God's will" to comfort another? Little more than "This is not my responsibility, thank God!"—and this to a brother or sister for whom Christ died.

SECOND LESSON: I CORINTHIANS 15:50-58

Those who have experienced some of the apostle's theological reasoning as a bit of a burden will find reconciliation and release in these magnificent

EIGHTH SUNDAY AFTER THE EPIPHANY 55

words. Verse 50 is a pivot between two sections. The lectionaries that repeat it from the previous Sunday reap the advantages of its "swing position." For Paul the resurrection is transformation to the supernatural realm, to the realm of God. His questions included (1) How can believers inherit the kingdom of God? and (2) What of those who have died? Both of these have pastoral implications and thus require theological rumination.

Paul is an apocalyptic theologian, but he has no interest in developing anthropomorphic pictures of life in heaven or hell. Some will die, but not all. What all shall share in common is transformation into a new body. Individualism motivates us to read the "body" of vv. 53-54 as new bodies. The apostle may have here, as elsewhere, the body of Christ in mind and view resurrection as the overcoming of multiplicity and diversity through the final perfection of the body into one. In any case, the "mystery," the apocalyptic secret, is that all will be radically altered. At that moment the apparently impermeable barrier that separates the living from the dead will collapse, like the wall of a besieged city that has fallen under an attack. Attacks were then prompted by trumpets. This will be the last trumpet, the sound that brings conflict to an end. This image of v. 52, like that of a heavenly garment in v. 53, are used without elaboration. The mixing of metaphors—sound the trumpet for battle and put on your party clothes—effectively evokes the discontinuity he proclaims. For both those who wish the prize of bodily continuity and those eager to shuffle off the mortal coil so that their immortal souls may enjoy uninhibited bliss, these words are a bit of a disappointment. Resurrection will disappoint our fondest dreams by giving us more than we can imagine.

The argument is bolstered with scriptural citations, no less impressive for the difficulty of identifying precise sources. Isaiah 25:8 and Hos. 13:14 are chief among these. Rather than speak of Satan, Paul, as in v. 26, prefers personified Death. This is a metonymy of sorts for Satan, but also more inclusive and less "mythological," a truly universal image of a universal human experience, one that transcends the limits of every culture and mode of thought. There is no room for hell, in the sense of eternal punishment, in 1 Corinthians 15. The victory is present. Although the wall and barrier of death and grave now separate the living from the dead, death has been defeated, granting rest for the departed and to the living grace and the possibility of new life. Death has lost its "sting," the goad used to keep people in line as if they were cattle and the bitterness that casts gloom upon every human aspiration and hope. We are not in heaven, but neither are our lives under the hegemony of that grim taskmaster, death. This is adequate grounds for thanksgiving (v. 57). The entire passage is a doxology. Well, one may say, "all psalms end with glory." The refrain here is "(not) in vain"

(vv. 10, 14, 58). For Paul the resurrection of Christ is "vain" if it is not the power that gives us victory. So he follows a long indicative of fifty-seven verses with a few short imperatives that are also prayers for his people. Neither his (v. 14) nor their "work" (v. 58) is worthless, for they have been endowed with the apostolic message of hope.

One way to exploit this text is as "background" to the Gospel, which speaks of the vanity of building without a foundation. If the Sermon seems to prescribe impossible imperatives, 1 Corinthians sets forth the indicative that makes it grace, not "law," conceived as the goad wielded by the wagonmaster of fate. Like houses built upon rock, believers can be steadfast and immovable because they are being made into living stones by the One strong enough to demolish the wall of death. They can do more than be steadfast and hold on. They can excel (v. 58).

GOSPEL: LUKE 6:39-49

Paul concludes 1 Corinthians 15 with an exhortation to excellence. One disadvantage of an egalitarian society—the advantages are numerous—is suspicion of the pursuit of excellence. Awards, raises, prizes, and honors can be poker chips in the game of power. The concomitant danger is that all will find it prudent to pursue mediocrity. In such a milieu the Sermon on the Plain is truly countercultural. The Christian doctrine that all are equal in the sight of God and no one is better than anyone else is not intended to imply anarchy or mediocrity. God's love for us makes the pursuit of excellence a genuine possibility for new life rather than a means of slipping into the kingdom by the skin our of teeth while grinding up the also-rans.

The climax to this Sermon of Jesus has three sections: vv. 39-42, vv. 43-45, and vv. 46-49. All relate to the theme of judgment, from human and divine perspectives. The reasoning is clear, the images apt, and the conclusion self-evident. Verses 39-42 engage leadership and the direction of others. Round one seems to go to the egalitarians. These verses do indicate that general human blindness makes it difficult to claim that hierarchical ranking is a quick solution to community problems. 1 Corinthians 12–14 exhibits kindred warnings. The opening question elicits but one answer: no. The great difficulty of this passage is the use to which it has been put. Since all have logs in their eyes, none may serve as directors. The result of this understanding is personal and communal paralysis. Growth under such conditions is not highly likely. The conclusion does suggest that logs can be removed, making vision and correction possible. In short, "Physician, heal yourself!" (Luke 4:23). Leaders must first and constantly attend to and take into account their personal faults, weaknesses, and growing edges. It is worth adding that they should also, as the closing parable suggests, recognize and build upon their strengths. Verse 40 applies the image of v. 39 to education, formation, with the object of making students "like teachers." When teachers do not understand this preposition, the result is that only superficial or narrow likenesses become the object of imitation. The more general application in vv. 42-43 exemplifies what this imitation means. Students, too, are to engage in self-examination as the first step of any action, in particular those requiring relations with others. The sequence is "Ready. Aim. Fire!" Those with logs in their eyes are not ready and cannot aim. They fire first, then aim, and presume that they are ready to move on to the next target. This famous passage does not say that we must never fire because we cannot ever see to aim, but that firing requires getting ready and taking careful aim: reflection and prudence. The blind do not presume to lead others who are blind because this is the luck of the draw, but because they do not realize that they are blind. The good news of the Sermon, announced in 4:18, is "recovery of sight to the blind." That recovery is a new way of seeing, the vision of God.

The structure of vv. 43-45, rather like that of Sir. 27:4-7, involves the repetition of parallel sayings. Here the point is made positively and negatively, to drive it home. Those who look for figs among thorns or grapes from bramble bushes are blind indeed. These homely proverbs gain their power from their overwhelmingly obvious truth. When applied to human beings, they make everything look simple. By their words (and deeds) people expose and thus judge themselves. There are problems here, for people are more deceptive than the most beguiling of poison fruits. This is why vv. 39-42 precede. Judgment is impaled on the horns of transparent clarity and impenetrable obscurity.

There is, and has been, many a sermon on the question of v. 46, a question parallel to that of v. 39. The social context is that lords had slaves. The primary requirement imposed upon the latter was obedience. Jesus says that too many are happy to be slaves when the dinner bell rings but neglect his order to go out in the fields. No work, no crop, and pretty soon no bread on the table.

At its end the Sermon returns to its beginning, with the threat and promise implicit in the parable corresponding to the overt promise and threat of beatitude and woe. When compared to Matt. 7:24-27, the closing parable of the Sermon on the Plain reflects appropriate "inculturation," for it suits a non-Palestinian environment. Such parables are typical conclusions to wisdom collections (cf. Prov. 9:13-18). The introduction to the parable speaks of "hearing" (cf. v. 27 and note that concordance). One is offered a choice: Upon what kind of foundation do you wish to build? The answer is easy, but then so is saying "Lord, Lord" (or, for that matter, "the temple of the LORD, the temple of the LORD, the temple of the LORD"). This Sermon has done more than advocate the benefits of a good foundation. Foundations are not easy to discern, for what looks solid may turn out otherwise. The Sermon is a course in spiritual engineering, short in length but comprehensive enough to treat both the beams from which buildings are fashioned and the specks of dust that can ruin precision equipment.

Products of this curriculum have learned new ways to see and hear, learning that is power to transform every sort of social interaction and to inject into every transaction the potential for novelty. The graduates have learned tactics for that which can alter every system of power. By turning the other cheek we give opportunity for others to knock beams from both our eyes and theirs; by handing our shirts as well to those who demand our jackets we reveal that the one without clothes is the emperor; by giving to those who ask we may well be grafting healthy branches onto rotten trees. What do spiritual engineers build? A house, not a room or a cell, but a dwelling for a family, the household of faith.

Fine, one may say, but where does Jesus, who reviled Pharisees and excoriated scribes, act out these words? This is a good question, not least for those who read the Sermon in a manner that is both sentimental and concrete. From this inconsistency we can learn that so-called "literal interpretation" of the Sermon is but one way of avoiding its challenge. If these injunctions were that simple, one would be justified in waiting until each cheek had been slapped before blasting an opponent to kingdom come. That kingdom does in some manner come when people dig deeply into these words. And the question? Holy Week, when Jesus is slapped, stripped, and deprived of life itself, will provide one answer—the final answer, as it happens.

The Transfiguration of Our Lord
Last Sunday after the Epiphany

Lectionary	First Lesson	Psalm	Second Lesson	Gospel
Revised Common	Exod. 34:29-35	Psalm 99	2 Cor. 3:12—4:2	Luke 9:28-36, (37-43)
Episcopal (BCP)	Exod. 34:29-35	Psalm 99	1 Cor. 12:27—13:13	Luke 9:28-36
Roman Catholic	Dan. 7:9-10, 13-14	Ps. 97:1-2, 5-6, 9	2 Peter 1:16-19	Luke 9:28-36
Lutheran (LBW)	Deut. 34:1-12	Ps. 99:1-5	2 Cor. 4:3-6	Luke 9:28-36

The *Lutheran Book of Worship* celebrates the transfiguration on the Sunday before Ash Wednesday. The *Book of Common Prayer* retains August 6 as the Feast of the Transfiguration, but always assigns to this Sunday transfiguration propers. For the latter this remains a Sunday in "Ordinary Time," but there are good reasons for "doing it up in white," less as the conclusion to a festive season that began at Christmas than to provide a contrast with Lent.

FIRST LESSON: DEUTERONOMY 34:1-12; EXODUS 34:29-35

Deuteronomy 34:1-12 (*LBW*). Deuteronomy 34 concludes not only that book but the entire Torah. Moses once again ascends a mountain, this time for a "Pisgah view" of the promised land, a land he is not destined to reach. The promise is already ancient, made to Abraham long ago. This panoramic vision is the culmination of his life. Great as he was, the title that holds first place is "servant of the LORD." An element of mystery enshrouds his death and burial, leaving him "available," as it were, for other activities. After this brief savor of the numinous, the narrative postpones its eulogy until it gives assurance of proper succession. So Elisha would succeed Elijah, whose departure from earth was even more mysterious and dramatic than that of Moses. One may note that both Elijah and Moses appear at the transfiguration. Moses was more than a lawgiver. He was superlative in prophecy and wonder-working as well. Intrabiblical competition with Elijah may be suspected. One result never intended by ancient Hebrew editors was the impetus this eulogistic summary would have upon Christology, in particular the Christology of Luke.

This reading evokes in a very different way from Exodus 24 the "bittersweet" character of the transfiguration, which hints of cross while displaying glory. Whereas transfigured Jesus is the object of sight, Moses is the subject of a vision. Yet the promised land is not for him. His work is over. Successors must now pick up the torch. In speech and narration the passage embraces all of salvation history to that point, from Abraham and Sarah to Joshua and his mainly nameless followers. Moses went directly from the mountain of vision to the valley of death. Jesus is about to make a similar journey.

Exodus 34:29-35 (*BCP*/Revised Common). This reading provides context for the transfiguration of Jesus, establishing him as a figure who had brought back the good old days of Moses, and/or one who was in direct communion with God. The account has a certain almost humorous quality (exploited by Paul in 2 Corinthians 3). Moses, who had neglected to look in a mirror before returning to his charges, was glowing. The history-of-religions background is the view that the essence of deity is a pure light, of which earthly light is but a pale imitation. Those who experience the sight or vision of God reflect this light upon their faces. The result is not admiration of Moses, but fear that contact with the divine will endanger mere mortals (cf. Exod. 19:10-25). Out of pastoral concern Moses resorts to the use of a veil. In this depiction Moses is strongly distinguished from the rest of the people, even Aaron and other leaders, becoming something of a divine being. Nonetheless, he took no credit for this achievement and did not seek to exploit it.

Artists have utilized several models over the centuries and millennia to depict this experience, including unusually bright faces, with raptured, upward-gazing eyes, and, most commonly, the halo. When Jerome revised the Latin Bible, he rendered the Hebrew as "horn," providing the grounds for Michelangelo's famous statue. This is all quite primitive, if charming. The passage deserves a hearing in an age that has, not without some good reasons, removed the sense of religious awe to the periphery. *Mysterium tremendum* can reduce the worshiping body into a collection of individuals isolated by fear of the sacred. At the peak of religious and liturgical renewal in the 1960s it sometimes seemed that the Dance of the Seven Veils had taken the place once held by decorous Moses. The times seem ripe for a recapture of some of that mystery, without its paraphernalia and piety. Despite the glorification of Moses here, his transfiguration was more of an obstacle, indeed a nuisance, than anything else. The holy can be a nuisance, but holy it remains. If for some the longing for the holy is a desire for some kind of possibly superficial thrill, for many others it represents a genuine quest for the transcendent. For all mystery is vital insofar as it proclaims that God and the ways of God lie beyond us. Leaders and preachers cannot always bring truth or even understanding. Very often we can only invite and

THE TRANSFIGURATION OF OUR LORD

assist people to be still and know the presence of God. The veil worn by Moses says that even the delivery of the Torah did not show all that God had to reveal. The primitive may be primitive, but it is no less potent for that.

SECOND LESSON: 2 CORINTHIANS 4:3-6; 1 CORINTHIANS 12:27—13:13

2 Corinthians 4:3-6 (*LBW*). 2 Corinthians is for many the most difficult of Paul's letters. Unraveling the order of this composite document provides some clarity, but the chief difficulty is that Paul seems to be arguing *against* positions he had so brilliantly established in 1 Corinthians. From this comes his reputation as an opportunist. A more profound approach will recognize the situational, that is, pastoral, character of his dialectic and seek the coherence that underlies his approach. In 3:7-18 the apostle appears to be poking fun at the story of Moses' transfiguration (Exod. 34:29-35). His motive was not, of course, general skepticism, but apparently the claim that this was the standard for authentic proclaimers, that genuine apostles should be able to demonstrate their credentials by "transfiguring" both text and self. Exegesis was a kind of striptease that would remove the veil from archaic texts (2 Cor. 3:13, 15). The means was evidently allegorical exposition, attended by the charismatic phenomenon of an altered countenance—probably glowing eyes (cf. Acts 6–7, esp. 6:15; 7:55). Paul's ire stems from his conviction that the church should not take its criteria for authenticity from the religious marketplace. The reason for this is that God does not choose to be bound to such criteria. Exhibit A is the cross, which also shows the coherence of Pauline theology. In 1 Corinthians the cross as divine wisdom judges earthly wisdom. 2 Corinthians uses the cross to criticize a theology of glory that has no place for the cross as apostolic credential and community sign.

His opponents maintained that he had hid the light of the gospel under the bushel basket of the cross. It was "veiled." If this is true, v. 3 maintains, the obscurity reveals that those who cannot see it are blind to the possibility that God might not follow their rules. Verse 4's "the god of this world" takes the argument almost as far as Marcion would. This god is a worldly product, but no less real for all of that. Those who proclaim a god that meets their expectations of what is true and fair are proclaiming themselves rather than God. In a narcissistic age (ruled by what Paul would call "the god of this world," the god of self) the valid desire of clergy to reveal their humanity issues in a great deal of self-proclamation. In terms of interest this runs up against the difficulty that my autobiography is fascinating, while yours is dull. There is a second difficulty: Christian preachers are charged with the proclamation of Christ, not of themselves.

Playing upon a theme of Satan as jealous of Adam and Eve, who were formed in God's image, Paul can refute an implicit "natural theology" by joining the creator God of Genesis 1 to the redeemer revealed in Christ. Marcion would find no comfort there. "Old" and new creation may not be as contiguous as some would wish, but the same God is responsible for both. New light shines "in our hearts" rather than upon our faces. This is not to say that it is a purely internal or emotional phenomenon. This light energizes apostles who can save while suffering. From the "worldly" perspective they look like failures, as, come to think of it, did Jesus. If Paul were critical of a pre-Gospel tradition of the transfiguration of Jesus (and others), there is a certain tension between this reading and the Gospel, when the latter is considered in isolation. 2 Corinthians 4:3-6 is less a text for a sermon than food for preachers, because, with intelligent reflection, this pericope will be of great assistance in the proclamation of the transfiguration in its Christian and, on this day, liturgical context. Transfiguration is revelation, not of a wonderful moment Jesus shared with some fortunate disciples, but of a new and different kind of light.

1 Corinthians 12:27—13:13 (*BCP*). *(For comments on this reading, see the Fourth Sunday after the Epiphany, above.)* Episcopalians who mourn the departure of the old pre-Lent "Gesima" Sundays will find here a residue of that tradition, as 1 Corinthians 13 was read on the Sunday before Lent. It continues to serve that purpose well by describing the spiritual growth toward which Lent calls us. Within the present setting, the *agape* eulogized by Paul is the power that can transfigure the world. All other transformations and metamorphoses are dim and imperfect, vague glimpses of the sort then viewed in mirrors made of polished metal.

GOSPEL: LUKE 9:28-36, (37-43)

Luke's account of the transfiguration is the most congenial of the Synoptic reports for this occasion, because this evangelist makes explicit links between this story and the passion-resurrection. The liturgical intent of reading this passage on the last Sunday before Lent is to look through that season to its climax: Holy Week and Easter.

The story of the transfiguration is certainly an epiphany, the manifestation of Jesus' divine nature. Some of the classic motifs, mountain, cloud, and light, appear here, quite transfigured themselves, as is the sound, no thunder now, but audible words. The original home of this story was probably an Easter story. The canonical tradition downplayed epiphanic aspects of the Risen One in favor of those that displayed continuity, as epiphanies seemed docetic. Some of these potentially docetic accounts were trans-

THE TRANSFIGURATION OF OUR LORD 63

ferred to pre-Easter locations (for example, Mark 6:45-52). The transfiguration may once have climaxed a collection of miracles that showed Jesus as a new Moses, leading his people across the water (Mark 4:35-41), feeding them in the wilderness (Mark 6:30-44), and, finally transformed upon a mountain. The canonical tradition has kept the elements but fashioned a new narrative. Another religiohistorical context is the Feast of Tabernacles, Succoth, motifs from which have colored the account, most notably in the "dwellings" of v. 33. Luke stimulates this association with his mysterious opening reference to "eight days" (cf. 2 Macc. 2:12). In the Christian tradition eight is the number of ultimate perfection and rest.

Greater weight must be laid upon the next prepositional phrase: "after these sayings." The sayings in question are Jesus's prediction of his death and resurrection. This context is fundamental. The epiphany is not a public event. Only a select company of disciples share the vision, and their perception is limited. Luke reports the transfiguration as another "prayer scene." Were it not so familiar, the sequence would be astonishing. The face and garments of Jesus change. The narrator states this absolutely. The following words come from the viewpoint of the disciples. "Two men," equally glorified, suddenly appear. They are, of course, Moses and Elijah. As two men they link this scene to the resurrection and the ascension (Luke 24:4; Acts 1:10). Luke also reports the subject of conversation. It was not the weather, but his "departure," a rich and ambiguous Greek word, *exodos*. To make this connection even more explicit and inclusive of the disciples, Luke borrows from Gethsemane the motif of their sleep, in this case exhaustion that is barely vanquished.

Just as the party, so to speak, was breaking up, Peter intervenes with what seems to be a perfectly reasonable proposal for a building program that will make of this unusual meeting an enduring celebration of Tabernacles. How could such an idea be misplaced? Because the journey is not yet finished, because cross precedes crown and suffering joy. This common attitude is just that with which Paul was at odds in the readings from 1 Corinthians that have recently occupied us. The disciples, too, must fall under the shadow of the cloud, no less the mystery of the passion than a fearful mark of God's presence. "Overshadowing" evokes the annunciation (Luke 1:35). There is another announcement, evocative of the baptism (Luke 3:22), but clearly addressed to others here ("This is" vs. "You are"). Luke prefers the epithet "chosen," which evokes Isa. 42:1 and the Servant's role as "light to the nations." This is the kind of epiphany to which the transfiguration points. The voice has some advice: "Listen to him." Among things to which they and we might listen are the immediately adjacent predictions, the parables of chap. 8, and, oh yes, the Sermon on the

Plain. This is another good occasion for examining "listen" (*akouein*) in Luke. Ancient heroes, blazing light, dazzling cloud, and striking voice having left, "Jesus was found alone." This is not the last time he will be alone.

The Revised Common addition of vv. 37-43 underlines the point. The Gospel is not yet finished. More than one-half of the story, and that not the least important part of it, remains. They come down from the mountain to find business as usual, if not worse. Satan has not thrown in the towel. Why do we ascend the mountain, if things are no better when we come down? For a "Pisgah view" of the promised land (*LBW* lectionary), for a view of the unity of God's saving plan (Moses, Elijah, and Jesus), for strength to take on evil in all of its forms. The demon of vv. 37-43 is exorcised, after all. Mountaintop moments are less relief from tedium and banality than medicine for weary souls, strength for the journey that is to come. Transfiguration does not blot out evil. In one of God's ironies the proper date of this Feast is August 6, the anniversary of another apparition of strange new light over Hiroshima. Transfigured Jesus would suffer no less later for his moment of glory now. As it comes to us in the Gospels, following a most brutal and disconcerting prediction and preceding a fateful journey to Jerusalem, transfiguration does not proclaim that evil has been vanquished by glory. It holds out the promise of God's ultimate victory and the possibility of seeking to transfigure evil, to fashion from bad motives and imperfect plans outcomes that can, with the grace of God, be good. Refreshed with this vision we, too, are ready for the road, the journey to Jerusalem. That journey, too, is food and preparation. We call it Lent. The heavenly embers that blazed on the mountain will, in three days, be ashes, ashes that God will fashion into new fire, the light and life of Easter.